Journey to and through the Second Death

J. Philip Scranton

xulon PRESS

Journey to and through the Second Death
by J. Philip Scranton

Printed in the United States of America

ISBN 978-1-60477-324-8

In most translations of the Bible the translators are free to use a range of synonyms for each word of the biblical languages. The Concordant Version makes a great effort to restrict the use of English words to what is deemed the most suitable English equivalent and those variations necessary for acceptable idiom. This results in what is probably the most *consistent* English version available. The new Dabhar Translation, "The Writ" is a work of similar nature, but it is somewhat less sensitive to idiom. The CV is not the smooth "easy read" that some versions are, but it has many great qualities that will endear it to the discerning student of the scriptures. Views expressed in this book may not be those of the Concordant Publishing Concern.

www.xulonpress.com

Dedication:

Special thanks to Donna for patient, understanding, long-term support. Thanks to unnumbered students of the Word who have gone before and found ways to leave their meditations behind. And thanks to my critics, the antagonistic as well as the sympathetic, for sharpening my focus.

JOURNEY TO AND THROUGH THE SECOND DEATH

Outline of Contents

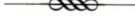

REDISCOVERING THE FIRST DEATH

The First Big Question

The most overlooked and most pertinent question in the study of the second death should be the most obvious: What is the *first* death? And then, is the second death a repetition of the first death? Unless the first death is defined, we can hardly define the second. Immediately an objection arises, "But we *know* death! Do we need to define it? It took Grandpa and Grandma from us. Then it tore away Dad and Mom, taking with them pieces of us. It's the price our blessed Savior had to pay to save us. We know death. We've heard of it since we were young, and we've seen its handiwork. And we know it is waiting till its time is right to take us." But, living in an age of which the Bible says Satan is god (2 Cor. 4:4), can we be sure we know what the true God has said about death? Humanity struggles to grasp the full truth in any field of endeavor. In Christianity alone there are several prominent views of death, all of which claim the Bible as their origin and authority. Many branches of Christianity use the second death as part of their definition for the first death. Can we be sure the truth about death has been dropped in our laps? Mass media vies for a position of influence, broadcasting shows that feature haunted houses, *near death* experiences and mediums who communicate with dead people, who are depicted as conscious, struggling with decisions, and even making choices to determine their destiny. Do we know death?

Dealing with Deception

Death has always been a cloudy issue for humanity. The book of Genesis opens with a death that brings a curse on all humanity. The New Testament opens with a death that removes the curse from humanity. Immediately linked to both of these deaths is the deception of the Adversary. In Genesis the deception was, "Ye shall not surely die," (Gen. 3:4 AV). And in the New Testament the deception was, He did not really rise. "His disciples came by night, and stole Him away," (Matt. 28:13 AV). The truth about death proclaims the importance of resurrection. The Adversary deceives us about death, and this deception about death causes us to misapprehend the resurrection of Christ and to misunderstand the second death. Christ's death was for the sins of the world. That fact alone, when fully realized makes His resurrection the spring of incessant rejoicing.

Unveiling the Resurrection

The resurrection of Jesus Christ is an indispensable element of the gospel. Christ alone has been raised to immortality. The resurrection marks God's approval on the work, life and identity of Christ (Rom. 1:4). The resurrection of Christ specifies Him as the One by Whom God will judge all the inhabitants of earth and the One in Whom faith should be vested (Acts 17:31). Christ's resurrection is the dawning rays of both hope and judgment. The resurrection of Jesus Christ is the verification of the justification of believers (Rom. 4:25), and therefore part of the basis of peace with God in grace (Rom. 5:1-2). The resurrection of Jesus Christ is an astonishing revelation of God's glory (Rom. 6:4, etc.).

The resurrection of Jesus Christ is a trumpet blast to humanity. It cannot be ignored. Man may try to ignore it. He may say it never happened. He may delay decisions about how he will respond to it. But the great equalizer, death, is coming. And when we realize death is circling *our* house, when we realize it is keeping vigil by *our* bed, then the fact that only One has ever returned from the grave, garbed in immortality, must be reckoned with. When our confidence in the flesh fails, and it will fail, only the questions about Jesus are worth answering, "Why did Jesus Christ rise from the dead? What was special about Him? How did He escape the clutches of death? What must I do to become like Him?" The resurrection of Jesus Christ demands a response from every individual who is aware of the reality of death.

Much of the biblical teaching about death prevalent today is based on selections in the Bible in which the primary subject is something other than death. The parable of the rich man and Lazarus, the promise to the repentant thief on Golgotha, and the Father's house in John 14 are prime examples. Armed with misunderstandings of these passages, students of the scriptures have forced complying interpretations on other passages where death *is* the primary topic.

What a person believes about death colors and controls what can be believed about resurrection. If a person believes that death is an unconscious condition, then the return of Christ and resurrection are of pre-eminent importance. These events initiate life and fellowship with God and bring us into glory. Resurrection ends death, liberating us from the clutches of the enemy. On the other hand, belief that death ushers us into heaven makes the resurrection and presence of

Christ events of only secondary importance that apparently provide some vague enhancement to an already blissful condition. Such beliefs cripple the believer's expectation in Christ's presence in the air and the resurrection.

If a believer goes directly to heaven upon dying, then he or she goes without a body. The body remains in the grave awaiting resurrection and glorification. Though the spirit returns to God (Lk. 23:46), that is no basis to assume it enjoys a conscious existence with Him. When Solomon said the spirit returns to God, his next line was, "Vanity of vanities,...the whole is vanity" (Eccl. 12:8). The spirits of animals return to God too (Ps. 104:29, 30), but that does not mean all the animals that have ever died are consciously in God's presence.

If a believer went directly to the presence of Christ at death, then ghosts, who are waiting for bodies, surround the Son of God. But Christ's resurrection was "out from among the dead" (1 Cor. 15:12, 20). Christ has been raised to immortality, a life unique to Him. He dwells in light so resplendent and glorious humans cannot behold Him, much less have access to Him (1 Tim. 6:16). How regrettable it is that believers honor death, the mortal wound of Satan, as their escort to Christ's presence.

If the lost go directly into torment, they have no body in which to experience torment, and they are sentenced before they are judged. If God torments before He judges or passes sentence, then God is unjust, and the coming of Christ is robbed of much of its import.

Death under the Sun

Was the writer of Ecclesiastes wrong? "All that your hand finds to do, do with your vigor, for there is no doing or devising or knowledge or wisdom in the unseen [*sheol*, or grave] where you are going" (Eccl. 9:10). He clearly states that death is a condition in which there is no consciousness. Yet we might be swayed to the popular opinion that this is only the viewpoint "under the sun," if not for the other, numerous, supporting testimonies. The Psalmists said, "For in death there is no remembrance of You," (Ps. 6:5); "The dead cannot praise Yah, nor all those descending into stillness" (Ps. 115:17). John wrote, "And no one has ascended into heaven except He Who descends out of heaven, the Son of Mankind Who is in heaven" (Jn. 3:13). On Pentecost, long after Christ's ascension, Peter said, "David did not ascend into the heavens," (Acts 2:34). None of these biblical writers place dead believers in heaven or a condition of consciousness.

When Do We Meet the Lord?
I Thessalonians 4:13-18

13 Now we do not want you to be ignorant, brethren, concerning those who are reposing, lest you may sorrow according as the rest, also, who have no expectation. 14 For, if we are believing that Jesus died and rose, thus also, those who are put to repose, will God, through Jesus, lead forth together with Him. 15 For this we are saying to you by the word of the Lord, that we, the living, who are surviving to the presence of the Lord, should by no means outstrip those who are put to repose, 16 for the Lord Himself will be descending from heaven with a shout of command, with the voice of the Chief Messenger, and with the trumpet of God, and the dead in Christ shall be rising first. 17 Thereupon we, the living who are surviving, shall at the same time be snatched away together with them in clouds, to meet the Lord in the air. And thus shall we always be together with the Lord. 18 So that, console one another with these words.

Verse 13 clearly states that this context treats the subject of believers who have died. Surviving brothers and sisters need not mourn to the degree, or in the same way as those who mourn the loss of loved ones apart from faith in Christ.

Verse 14 is poorly rendered by most English versions. *Sleeping in Jesus* is a poor representation of the original language and thought, and it is suggestive of thoughts foreign to the context. The "in" is actually "through". Is Paul speaking here of some who have died "through Jesus?" Is he speaking of martyrdom, or saying that Christ is responsible for their death? Not at all. The "through" is misplaced. Some believers died, and God will, "through Jesus," bring them forth! One further comment on this verse is necessary. The phrase "with Him", is only "Him" in the original. The word "with" is supplied, and cannot be construed to mean that the believing dead are "with Christ," in the sense of being in His presence. And the rest of the passage confirms the believing dead do not return from heaven with Christ at His coming.

In verse 15 Paul assures the Thessalonians that the believing dead will not be overlooked or left behind—the living believers will not precede them in meeting Christ. Clearly the Thessalonians did not think the believing dead were already with Christ—they feared they would be irrevocably lost if they did not live until Christ's presence!

Verse 16 tells that the first step in the presentation of the body of Christ to their Lord is the raising to life of the believers who have died. No one meets the Lord while being dead.

Verse 17 says that once the dead believers are raised to life, then the living believers shall, "at the same time," be snatched away together with the resurrected believers "**to meet** the Lord". Whether believers die long before the Lord returns, or whether they live until He comes, **they all meet the Lord at the same time**.

The word translated "same time" means *simultaneous*. This word was used in the parable of the wheat and tares in Matthew 13:29. The tares were not to be pulled or weeded out from among the wheat before the harvest, because it would be impossible to remove the one without uprooting the other *at the same time*. The roots of the two plants were so intermingled that they could not be separated. If one left the soil, the other was going to leave the soil simultaneously. Believers who have died do not meet the Lord when they die. They do not go to be with Him until the resurrection. They will meet the Lord simultaneously with those believers who are alive at Christ's return.

Verse 18 says, "And thus shall we always be together with the Lord…." "Thus," meaning, in this way, or, by these events coming to pass, shall we be together with the Lord. This is the message of hope that is to be used to comfort the bereaved.

The Prerequisite of Glory
1 Corinthians 15:50-55

50 Now this I am averring, brethren, that flesh and blood is not able to enjoy an allotment in the kingdom of God, neither is corruption enjoying the allotment of incorruption.
51 Lo! a secret to you am I telling! We all, indeed, shall not be put to repose, yet we all shall be changed, 52 in an instant,
in the twinkle of an eye, at the last trump. For He will be trumpeting, and the dead will be roused incorruptible, and we shall be changed. 53 For this corruptible must put on incorruption, and this mortal put on immortality.

54 Now, whenever this corruptible should be putting on incorruption and this mortal should be putting on immortality, then shall come to pass the word which is written,

Swallowed up was Death by Victory.

55 Where, O Death, is your victory?
Where, O Death, is your sting?

This passage supplies further details to the events outlined in 1 Thessalonians 4:13-18. But here Paul emphasizes the aspect of immortality. Verse 50 makes it unmistakably clear no one enters glory—no one goes to heaven—before these bodies of humiliation are changed. Corruption cannot enjoy the allotment of incorruption. Again, the sequence is the same as in Thessalonians. The dead will be raised in glorified bodies, and the living believers will be changed. With this changing comes our glory. With this changing we meet Christ. It is this victory over our death and mortality that brings us to Christ.

Paul's Logical Argument on the Resurrection
1 Corinthians 15:12-34

In the 15th chapter of 1 Corinthians, Paul battles doctrinal error with a fivefold argument concerning the resurrection. Each of the five theses of the argument is introduced by the phrase: *if there is no resurrection*, or by an equivalent thought. In speaking of the resurrection, he speaks also of death. And the things Paul says and insinuates regarding death show clearly that it is a condition that is void of consciousness.

I. But **if** there be no resurrection of the dead,
  A. **then** is Christ not risen
    1. And **if** Christ be not risen
      a. **then** is our preaching vain
      b. **and** your faith is also vain
  B. Yea, **and** we are found false witnesses of God, because we have testified of God that he raised up

Christ, whom he raised not up, if so be that the dead rise not. (vv. 13-15)

II. For **if** the dead rise not,
- A. **then** is not Christ raised;
  - 1. And **if** Christ be not raised,
    - a. [**then**] your faith is vain,
    - b. [**then**] ye are yet in your sins.
- B. **Then** they also who are fallen asleep in Christ are perished. (vv. 16-18)

III. **If** in this life only we have hope in Christ,
- A. [**then**]We are of all men most miserable. (v. 19; vv. 20-28 are parenthetical, so are omitted here.)

IV. Else what shall those be doing who are baptizing? **If** the dead are not being roused,
- A. [**then**]it [baptism] is for the sake of the dead absolutely. Why are they baptizing for their sake?
- B. [Why suffer persecution?] And why stand we in jeopardy every hour?...If after the manner of men, I have fought with beasts at Ephesus, what doth it profit me? (vv. 29-32)

V. **If** the dead rise not,
- A. [**then**] Let us eat and drink; for tomorrow we die. (v. 32)

VI. The conclusion of the matter:
- A. Be not deceived: Evil company corrupts good morals.
- B. Awake to righteousness and sin not, for some have not the knowledge of God.
- C. I speak this to your shame. (vv. 33-34)

(Quotations are from the Scofield version of the Authorized Version, except for verse 29 which is from the Concordant Version. Those familiar with the difficulties of this verse will appreciate this improved translation. The AV employs the repetitive use of *if* and *then* in such a way that it highlights the flow of thought in Paul's argument. It is quite helpful here. We have added **then** in brackets where it is understood.)

I. The first thesis covers verses 13-15. Simply stated, Paul says, **if** there is no resurrection, **then**: A. Christ has not been raised (which has the double result of negating any value in Paul's preaching and the Corinthian's faith), and, B. Paul would have been a false witness of God.

In Paul's **if** statement, the word *dead* is plural. Paul is referring to all the dead, not to the death of Christ alone. If no one will be raised from the dead, then Christ was not raised either, and everything that the believing Corinthians had experienced—the gifts of the Spirit, peace with God, fellowship and communion—was void. All that had happened to the Corinthians since the time Paul had come preaching was undeniably real to them. They had experienced the power of the message and the divine verifications of its truth.

The headship of Christ over humanity is asserted here. As Paul will show later in vv. 20-28, Christ's resurrection is inseparably joined with the resurrection of all humanity. He is the Firstfruit, the Firstborn from among the dead, and the Firstfruit stands for the whole harvest. None of humanity can be raised apart from Christ, and in His resurrection is the divine promise that all humanity will be raised.

Secondly, **if** the dead are not raised, **then** Paul and his associates were false witnesses of God. Is God able to raise the dead? Was God operating in Christ? To question the resurrection, and thereby the gospel of God, is to question both the power of God and the truth of the gospel. This is the sum of his first thesis of the argument.

II. "For **if** the dead rise not," (v. 16). Again Paul follows his *if* statement with two irrefutable results: A. Christ was not raised, leaving the Corinthians without salvation, still in their sins, because justification from sin is proven by Christ's resurrection (Rom. 4:25). This again refers to the headship of Christ. "For even as, in Adam, all are dying, thus also, in Christ, shall all be vivified" (1Cor. 15:22). Christ died for the sins of humanity (Jn. 1:29). All that was lost in Adam's disobedience is more than recovered in the obedience of Christ (Rom. 5:12-21), and the resurrection of Christ verifies that the sins He bore are completely resolved (Acts 17:30-31; Rom. 1:4; 4:25-5:2).

The second irrefutable result is: B. Believers who died have perished. The statement would read, "**If** the dead rise not, **then** believers in Christ who have died have perished." Of course some will object and say that the statement means that believers would perish in death only if Christ Himself were not raised. Again, the plurality of the word *dead* dismisses that objection. If there is no resurrection of the dead, any dead, then believer's who have died have perished.

What does the word *perished* say about the condition of the dead? It cannot be limited to the body alone, because the context includes the resurrection of Christ as well as that of believers. *Perished* cannot possibly describe a conscious existence in the presence of Christ, regardless of what many claim death to be.

And what does Paul say prevents believer's from being perished? Does he say that since they believed at some time during their life, believers who have died have not perished? No. Does he say that because believers who *have passed* are with Christ they have not perished? No. He says that, apart from the resurrection, believers who have died have perished. Believers who have died are awaiting the resurrection to free them from what would be a *perished condition*, if it were not for the resurrection.

III. "If in this life only we have hope in Christ," (v. 19). This is a variation of Paul's original thesis, "If there is no resurrection." Clearly it is the same thought. Hope in Christ limited to the present life is the same as having no resurrection. And listen to Paul's result! If there is no resurrection of the dead, believers are the most pitiful group of all humanity!

Why would this be true? It would be true because death would be the end of existence for believers. There is no blissful intermediate state for believing souls. Without resurrection a dead man is no better than a dead dog or a dead gnat. Only resurrection can bring back to life and consciousness.

Three times Paul has argued the incumbent consequences if there were no resurrection. He will bring that argument forward twice more, but the very thought, of no resurrection, is so distressing that he breaks forth into one of the most glorious passages of the Bible. "But now is Christ risen from the dead and become the first fruits of them that slept" (v.20). And on he goes until he can close with that most glorious and longed for consummation: "that God may be all in all" (v. 28). And ultimately his discussion of resurrection will conclude with an exclamation of victory, taunting Death! "Where, O Death, is your victory? Where, O Death, is your sting?...Thanks be to God, Who is giving us the victory, through our Lord Jesus Christ" (1 Cor. 15:55-57).

Paul's argument resumes in verse 29. IV. Paul's fourth thesis on the subject relates to baptism and the believer's daily life and testing of faith. Why would a person who had no hope of escaping the grave be baptized?! Remembering the Corinthian controversy over baptism (1:10-17 cf. also 10:2; 12:13), it is easily seen that Paul is trying to bring the importance of the resurrection home to his readers by using examples that were precious to them. Baptism pictures both death and resurrection. What a rebuke it was for Paul to ask the Corinthians this question! It is as if he said, "How can you be boasting that you were baptized by Apollos or baptized by Paul? You are saying there is no resurrection. And if there is no resurrection, then baptism is a picture of nothing and means nothing! What possible reason could you have for baptizing if you truly don't believe in resurrection?!" (1 Cor. 1:12-15; 15:29)

This he follows with the topic of persecution. Why would one lay down their life for the testimony of Christ, if there is no escape from the grave?! Or, to rephrase the thought, "It would be stupid to suffer persecution for the name of Christ, if there will not be a resurrection! If there is no resurrection, the believers who died at the jaws and claws of beasts in the Ephesian arena were fools! They died for nothing!"

These statements are so strong that two things must be said. First, there is no blessedness in death for the believer or anyone. Death is an enemy, the destruction of which we anticipate with great fervor. Second, the resurrection is misunderstood and belittled today. The resurrection is not honored with the emphasis and glory that it merits.

V. Paul's fifth thesis brings him to the close of the debate portion of his argument. If the dead will not be raised, eat and drink, for tomorrow you die! If there is no resurrection, take what enjoyment you can from life, for there is nothing in or beyond the grave.

Christ's resurrection is the promise that death will be abolished. Christ's resurrection marks the beginning of the new creation and the eradication of all the acts of the Adversary. Christ's resurrection is our hope and glory!

VI. Paul concludes his argument with an exhortation to correct the ills of this false teaching. He says three things, paraphrased here: (1) "Do not be deceived! The result of entertaining such teachings and teachers is corruption, both of faith and conduct." (2) "Wake up to the critical importance of the resurrection and do not miss the mark of truth in correcting this false teaching. This error springs from an ignorance of God and His word." (3) "I have carried this argument to the full degree that it merits. Perhaps you think I am extreme. But my purpose in doing so was to shame and embarrass you into doing what is right. The consequence is too great for me to take any chance of being misunderstood."

One more thought should be mentioned regarding this passage. Some will wish to redefine resurrection, and say the term can apply to an altered existence in an intermediate state. To be sure, we will be gloriously altered. But it is certain that resurrection must be to a conscious existence in a tangible body. 1 Corinthians 15 sets that truth forward in unmistakable terms.

At Home with the Lord
2 Corinthians 5:1-8

(1) For we are aware that, if our terrestrial tabernacle house should be demolished, we have a building of God, a house not made by hands, eonian, in the heavens. (2) For in this also we are groaning, longing to be dressed in our habitation which is out of heaven, (3) if so be that, being dressed also, we shall not be found naked. (4) For we also, who are in the tabernacle, are groaning, being burdened, on which we are not wanting to be stripped, but to be dressed, that the mortal may be swallowed up by life. (5) Now He Who produces us for this same longing is God, Who is also giving us the earnest of the spirit.

(6) Being, then, courageous always, and aware that, being at home in the body, we are away from home from the Lord (7) (for by faith are we walking, not by perception), (8) yet we are encouraged, and are delighting rather to be away from home out of the body and to be at home with the Lord.

Paul makes use of figurative expressions speaking of two homes, one terrestrial and one in the heavens. And he speaks of two bodies, which he contrasts, calling one a "terrestrial tabernacle house, and the other, a building of God, a house not made by hands, eonian, in the heavens" (2 Cor. 5:1).

Then Paul expands his figures and speaks of these bodies as clothing. In the earthly tabernacle body we are burdened and are groaning. But we are **not** wanting to be stripped of the body. Paul is very clear that he does not wish to be found naked, which would be the condition of being without the body, or dead. Far from that, he emphatically declares that he wants to be "dressed" (v. 4). He yearns for the terrestrial body to be swallowed up by life. He desires mortality to be overcome by immortality without ever passing into death.

With this in mind, when verse 8 is read, it is clear that Paul's desire "to be out of the body and to be at home with the Lord" (2 Cor. 5:8) is by no means a desire to die. It is a desire to be away from all the burdens and struggles of this life and to be enjoying the glories of the "habitation which is out of heaven" (v. 2). Paul did not believe that death offered any benefit at all. To be dead was to be naked, or stripped.

What Is Gain?
Philippians 1:20-24

(20) In accord with my premonition and expectation, that in nothing shall I be put to shame, but with all boldness, as always, now also, Christ shall be magnified in my body, whether through life or through death. (21) For to me to be living is Christ, and to be dying, gain. (22) Now if it is to be living in flesh, this to me means fruit from work, and what I shall be preferring I am not making known. (23) (Yet I am being pressed out of the two, having a yearning for the solution and to be together with Christ, for it, rather, is much

better.) (24) Yet to be staying in the flesh is more necessary because of you.

"For to me to be living is Christ, and to be dying, gain" (v. 21). This passage is frequently explained to mean that Paul believed martyrdom would usher him into the bliss of heaven. That view is wrong for several reasons. First, such a view is in disagreement with other statements by Paul, as noted above. Second, Paul is not interested in personal gain. It he lives, he lives to serve Christ. If he dies, he will be a martyr for the cause of Christ, and he expects his death to further the gospel. The gain Paul speaks of is gain for the cause of Christ. This thought is consonant with the earlier verses of the chapter, where he expresses his desire to be released from jail so he can evangelize. Yet he is rejoicing that his confinement has generated so much attention to his position that others are evangelizing because of his absence, and the total effect is a larger work than he could accomplish himself, if he were free.

The third reason this passage does not mean Paul expected death to bring him "gain", is because his desire is for a completely different solution. Paul clearly says that he will not reveal whether he thinks evangelizing or martyrdom is better. Instead, he is "pressed out of the two" (v. 23). He prefers neither evangelizing nor martyrdom. He prefers "to be together with Christ, for it, rather, is much better" (v. 23). Paul yearns for a third option. He yearns for Christ to return and change him. He yearns to be in the presence of Christ. He echoes the same sentiment here as in 2 Corinthians 5. And he lends no support to the idea that there is any bliss or benefit in death. In 1 Corinthians 15:32 Paul poses the question, "If I were to be killed by the beasts in the Ephesian arena, 'what is the benefit to me, if the dead are not being roused?'" Blessedness is dependent on the return of Christ and glorification, not on death.

The God of the Living
Matthew 22:31-32; Mark 12:26-27; Luke 20:37-38

The God of Abraham, Isaac, and Jacob is not the God of the dead, but of the living. Does this mean these patriarchs must currently be alive? No. In each of these passages it is clearly stated that their "living" is with respect to the resurrection. The patriarchs will be raised, because their God is the living God, and none of His will be endlessly bound by death. There is no insinuation that they are alive before their resurrection.

The Father's House

"In My Father's house are many abodes; yet if not I would have told you, for I am going to make ready a place for you. And if I should be going and making ready a place for you, I am coming again and I will be taking you along to Myself, that where I am, you also may be" (Jn. 14:2, 3).

This passage is frequently read at funerals in such a manner as to suggest that the dead have joined Christ and are now dwelling in a mansion that is part of the Father's house. Christ used the term *Father's house* in John 2:16 in reference to the temple in Jerusalem that was being built by Herod, not to a place of heavenly mansions. In the verses quoted Christ said that He would return and take His disciples to Himself. Clearly the disciples should be looking for the return of Christ if they wish to enter an abode that He has prepared for them. Christ said nothing here to insinuate that death would escort them to His presence.

A Grandstand of Faith?
Hebrews 11:39-12:1

What do the words, "we…having so vast a cloud of witnesses encompassing us" (12:1), mean? It is true we are a theater to the world around us and to the spiritual beings (1 Cor. 4:9), but this refers to the living observing the living. In Hebrews the "cloud" of those who had died in faith were witnesses, not because they were witnessing the living, but because their lives were an example of living in belief of the promises of God. The writer notes in 11:39, 40 that the faithful who have died have not entered into the promises and they will not be perfected apart from the faithful of the believers' day. The scriptures and history abound with examples of faithfulness. These examples testify to those who are living that the life of faith can and should be lived in expectation. That is the intent of the passage. Therefore, "putting off every impediment and the popular sin, [we] may be racing with endurance the contest lying before us," (12:1).

The Repentant Malefactor
Luke 23:43

It is frequently supposed the words of Christ from the cross to the repentant malefactor prove Christ went to heaven, or paradise, that very day, and took the malefactor with Him. In the Authorized Version it reads: "Verily I say unto thee, Today shalt thou be with me in paradise." The Concordant Version reads: "Verily, to you am I saying today, with Me shall you be in paradise." The difference between the two is significant. In the AV the time element is associated with paradise. In the CV the time element is associated with the promise. Christ was saying, "I am promising you today that you will (eventually) be with me in paradise." Christ was not saying, "I am promising you that you will be with Me in paradise today."

How do we vindicate this position? Christ had yet to spend three days and nights in the grave. On resurrection morning, when the Lord spoke to Mary in the garden, He said, "Not as yet have I ascended to My Father" (Jn. 20:17). The book of Revelation places the tree of life in the paradise of God (Rev. 2:7), which has yet to descend from God out of heaven (Rev. 21, 22). This places paradise in heaven with God. If Christ did not ascend to the Father until three days after His crucifixion, He could not have been in paradise the day of His crucifixion with the repentant malefactor. Again, "No one has ascended into heaven except He Who descends out of heaven, the Son of Mankind Who is in heaven" (Jn. 3:13). Even now, the repentant malefactor has not arrived in paradise. Eventually he will be there because of Christ's promise. We paraphrase that promise here: "Truly I am saying to you, because of what is happening on this day on which I am dying for your sins and those of the entire world, you will be with Me in paradise".

The Rich Man and Lazarus
Luke 16:19-31

It is frequently assumed, since both the rich man and Lazarus are said to die, their obvious consciousness in Abraham's bosom and hades proves the dead are conscious. Yet all the previously mentioned passages, which are vitally concerned with the subject of death, have shown the Bible's teaching to be contrary to what first may appear to be taught by this parable. Should this one parable, the point of which has nothing to do with literal death, upset the statements of many other passages of scripture? Or, instead, should poetic license be allowed the Great Storyteller if there seems to be a controversy?

And who, of those who insist this parable teaches the literal truth about death, is willing to apply other statements of this parable to the upsetting of other biblical teachings? Specifically, who believes and is willing to make verse 25 the basis for future bliss or agony? "Now Abraham said, 'Child, be reminded that you got your good things in your life, and Lazarus likewise evil things. Yet now here he is being consoled, yet you are in pain'" (Lk.16:25). Shall the churches teach that the way to future joy is through present poverty and agony? Shall we leave all earthly possessions, quit our jobs, become beggars, and infect ourselves with disease in order to have future happiness?

Neglect is insinuated on the part of the rich man, but where is any evidence of virtue in Lazarus? Perhaps he became a diseased beggar through drunken debauchery! Abraham's statement in verse 25 does not guarantee otherwise. And when we consider the context, it is easily seen that Christ did not intend for any spiritual virtue to be associated with Lazarus. Lazarus is representative of the publicans and sinners who were entering the kingdom before the Pharisees. Christ did not consider them virtuous, just needy.

Faith is not mentioned with respect to either of these characters in the parable. The key thoughts that are mentioned regarding them, such as Abraham's bosom, were Pharisaic traditions, not the teaching of the scriptures. The Pharisees continually criticized every detail of Christ's teaching. In this passage, He used their own catch phrases and pet views to capture their attention and challenge their thinking. And, while faith is not mentioned with reference to the two main characters, it is definitely a qualifying feature for the rich man's brothers (vv. 29-31). The purpose of this parable is to provide a setting for belief in the resurrection of Christ to become the determining factor for entering into bliss or torment—into kingdom blessing or exclusion from kingdom blessing.

Is This Passage a Parable?

Some have maintained this passage is not a parable and it must be understood as a literal account. There is, indeed, much widespread teaching on paradise and hell which stands, like an inverted pyramid, on literal interpretation of this passage. At first glance, the passage seems to specify "a certain rich man" and "a certain poor man named Lazarus". But the word used here for "certain" is *any* (*tis*), and it is English idiom—not definition—that requires the use of "certain." This word is commonly used in many parables, and especially in Luke (compare Matt. 21:33; 22:2; Lk. 7:41; 10:30, 31, 33; 12:16; 13:6; 14:16; 15:11; 16:1; 19:12; 20:9).

The use of the name "Lazarus" has also been a point of objection to viewing this passage as a parable. But the 23rd chapter of Ezekiel uses names in a parable, and the names in that parable have symbolic meanings, like Lazarus, which means *helpless*. Furthermore, the particular name of Lazarus in this parable is too prophetic to be coincidental. The whole passage (chapters 15 and 16) culminates in Christ's final statement: "If Moses and the prophets they are not hearing, neither will they be persuaded if someone should be rising from among the dead" (Lk. 16:31). Lazarus was raised from the dead (Jn. 11), and the Pharisees' counsel was that he too should be killed, along with Jesus. It is not unlikely that some of the Pharisees hearing this parable were among the company of those who were incensed at the raising of Lazarus. Lazarus' resurrection was the culminating sign of the Lord's ministry, and it did not convince the Jews, just as the parable prophesies here.

Luke's Theme

The 15th and 16th chapters of Luke form a discourse of five parables concerning the Pharisees and scribes and their murmuring at sinners drawing close to Christ (15:1-3; 16:14). One of the primary themes in Luke is the contrast between those who are *near* and those who are *afar off*. This theme springs up early in the book where the people are seen *outside* praying while the priest had *entered in* (1:9,10). The theme flows throughout the book and closes with the scene of continual praising and blessing of God *in the sanctuary* (24:53). This theme is especially relevant in Luke 15 and 16. Chapter 15 (the sheep, coins and sons) manifests the Father's joy in receiving those who are afar off into His bosom. Chapter 16 speaks of the obligations (stewardship, marriage and wealth) violated by those who should have been near.

In the story of the father with two sons, the younger son represents the sinners and tax collectors. He squanders all his inheritance in a *far country*, but, owning his worthless condition, he returns, and, *still being far away*, he is seen and received joyfully by his father. The father fondly embraces him *into his bosom*. The elder son, who had the right to all the father's possessions, and had been *near* all along, came *near* at the time of the prodigal's return but was self-righteously offended and would *not enter*.

The story line is very much the same with Lazarus and the rich man. Abraham is the father of both, just as he is the father of the Pharisees and the publicans and sinners. Wealth and prosperity was a sign of divine blessing in the era of Israel's covenant. The royal purple and priestly cambric are symbols of Israel as a reigning nation of priests, which will be their position when the promise to Abraham to be a blessing to all nations is fulfilled. Lazarus' poverty and ulcers are a symbol of the publicans' and sinners' uncleanness and social standing. The rich man was "daily making merry splendidly" (v. 19) with Pharisaic indifference, while Lazarus was *outside the gate*, wishing only for scraps of what lay within. The word *psichion,* scraps, is only used in two contexts—here (Lk. 16:21), and in the healing of the Syro-Phoenician woman's child (Matt. 15:27; Mk. 7:28). In both cases the scraps are symbolic of the remnants or crumbs of Israel's blessings as God's chosen. Lazarus is blessed to come *near*—into the very bosom of Abraham, but the rich man finds himself *outside* of blessing with an impassable chasm between.

Like the lepers of chapter 17, the tax collector and Bartimaeus of chapter 18, and Zacchaeus of chapter 19, Lazarus was *outside* or *afar off.* Like the Pharisees of chapter 15 who would not enter the house; the Pharisee of chapter 18 who prayed toward himself, the rich young man who went away sorrowful and the murmurers of chapter 19 who were disgruntled at Jesus' entry into Zacchaeus' house, the rich man was ultimately the one left outside.

Interpretation of the Parable

The primary difference between this parable and many of the others that Christ gave is the time period to which it applies. Like the wheat and tares, this parable applies to the first era of the kingdom. Since the rejection of Christ by Israel, believing Jews have rested in the bosom of faith, not yet receiving the promises, but waiting for them. The passing of generations makes the setting of hades appropriate. Israel's covenant is broken and the temple is gone. The nation as a whole has been tormented in the fires of anti-Semitism. Disbelief, even "if someone should be rising from the dead" (16:31), has doomed the rich man and his brethren. Israel's future reception back into God's favor will be "life from among the dead" (Rom. 11:15). This national death is figurative, just as the death in the parable is figurative. In God's purpose, the covenant with Israel had to be broken in order to do away with the law so that grace could reign. Now individuals, both of the nations and Israel, are being given faith apart from law.

Old Testament Prophecy and This Parable

There are two passages in the Old Testament which should be read and considered with this parable. They are Deuteronomy 32:10-26 and Jeremiah 5:27-29. These passages have remarkable similarities to this parable, and they support the interpretation given here.

Dives is Latin for *wealthy*, and is commonly given as the name of the rich man. We suggest a different name, *Jeshurun.* Jeshurun is a poetic name for Israel meaning *upright one*. It occurs in the Deuteronomy passage, which is also known as the song of Moses. Jeshurun grew fat and forsook his God. Like the obese Eli, who did not correct or control his sons, Israel luxuriated in the benefits of God and became distracted by the surrounding world. In jealous anger God gave them over to the nations. "For a fire will be kindled by My anger, and it shall glow unto the unseen [sheol] beneath; it shall devour the earth and its crop, and it shall set aflame the foundations of the mountains" (Deut. 32:22). This prophecy found repeated fulfillment in the calamities which befell unfaithful Israel at the hands of the nations.

The larger context for the Jeremiah passage is all of chapters 5 and 6. Jeremiah is told to condemn Israel, and especially Jerusalem, for their corruption. The punishment receives numerous descriptions, including fire, and was fulfilled by the Babylonian captivity.

"Therefore thus says the LORD, the God of hosts:...I am making my words in your mouth a fire, and this people wood, and the fire shall devour them. Behold, I am bringing upon you a nation from afar...

"Like a basket full of birds, their houses are full of treachery; therefore they have become great and rich, they have grown fat and sleek. They know no bounds in deeds of wickedness; they judge not with justice the cause of the fatherless, to make it prosper, and they do not defend the rights of the needy. Shall I not punish them for these things? says the LORD, and shall I not avenge myself on a nation such as this?" (Jer. 5:14, 15, 27-29 RSV).

Clearly these passages lay a foundation for the Lord's presentation of the parable. Christ Himself is the great summation of all spiritual wealth. Israel held that wealth typically, but lost it with the rejection of Christ. In Israel's rejection of Him all these passages find their greatest fulfillment. The death of a nation is represented in these passages, a death that leaves them as a valley full of dry bones, yet a nation to be raised or *reborn* later. It is a death like that of the prodigal: "your brother was dead and revives, and was lost and was found" (Lk. 15:32).

Why is it that five brothers would end up in torment? They would not believe either the testimony of the scriptures or the sign of resurrection. Why is it that the Jews have been persecuted throughout the world? Because they received not the testimony of the oracles of God which were committed to them, neither did they believe the sign of the prophet Jonah—the resurrection of Christ. Therefore, the birthright was lost by those who failed to exercise it in the character of the True Elder Brother. The blessing was passed to those who by faith are sons of Abraham.

Death and Faith

The Hebrew word *aron* means a *chest* or *box*. The first use of this word in the Bible is in Genesis 50:26 where it says that Joseph was placed in a *coffin* in Egypt. The next 135 plus occurrences of this word are translated *ark* (Authorized Version), and refer to the *ark* or *coffer* of the covenant which contained the stone tablets of the ten commandments. This is a different word than the one used for Noah's ark. Why did God introduce this word, which almost exclusively refers to the symbol of His covenant relation to Israel and the very seat of His communication with them, by using it to refer to Joseph's coffin? Curious too is the similarity between the way a coffin is carried, and the way God designed the coffer of the covenant to be carried.

It has been noted that the book of Genesis begins with the words "In the beginning God created..." and that it ends with the words, "...in a coffin in Egypt (AV)." By noting these words, emphasis was laid upon the ruin brought by sin and death. But the emphasis of Joseph's words, as he looked death in the eyes, was quite different. "I am dying. Yet visit, yea visit will the Elohim you, and bring you up from this land to the land which the Elohim swore to our forefathers, to Abraham, to Isaac, and to Jacob. And adjuring is Joseph the sons of Israel saying, Visit, yea visit you will the Elohim, and up shall you bring my bones with you" (Gen. 50:24-25). Joseph's outlook was one of faith. With unshakeable confidence he assured them that God would come to them and bring them into the land of promise. And with resolute determination he required of them a solemn promise to take his body with them. The carrying of Joseph's coffin to Canaan was a testimony to faith in God's promise.

How important were Joseph's faith and the oath he required of the sons of Israel to their deliverance? How much of the unity of the people and their commitment to leave did

God instill in them through the passing down from generation to generation of one man's faith? Throughout the wearisome years of slavery, how many times around an evening fire did someone speak of Joseph's promise that God would come for them and take them into a new land? And how many young ears heard and believed that God would someday come and deliver them? When the days finally came, how many hundreds thought, "We *must* take the coffin of Joseph with us."

When Moses led the children of Israel out of Egypt, they took Joseph's coffin with them (Ex. 13:19). Pall bearers were part of the procession through the wilderness. Pall bearers walked through the desert night guided by the light of a pillar of fire. Pall bearers walked through the heat of the day under the shade of a pillar of cloud. Pall bearers walked through the Red Sea and out on the other side, where Pharaoh and his chariots could not follow.

But before they reached Canaan, at Mt. Sinai, another set of bearers were designated to carry the symbol of God's promise and covenant with the nation. And in the coffer these bearers bore would be placed the stone tablets, the golden pot of manna and the rod of Aaron that budded—the things that represent Christ, His faith, His death, and His resurrection in the perfect fulfillment of the law.

Joseph had become the lawgiver and ruler of Egypt, having highest authority in the empire next to Pharaoh. He had made Egypt to become the house of bread that fed the world during a seven year long famine. In a typical sense Joseph had been raised from the dead twice—once when he was pulled up out of the pit or cistern where his brothers had thrown him, and a second time when he was delivered from prison.

It is not at all difficult to see Joseph as a wonderful representation or type of Christ. And the similarity between the coffer of the covenant and the coffin of Joseph is also easy to see. And how amazingly similar are the bones of Joseph in a coffin, when we think of all his life represented, to the contents of the coffer of the covenant. The lid of the coffer, sometimes called the mercyseat, was where the blood of the sin offering was placed, and it was the place from which God spoke and communed with His people. God stands on the faith and death of Christ, and from that ground He communes with us and guides us and rules us. Christ's death and faith are our shelter and our redemption.

Death, relentless, unyielding, implacable death, is the measuring stick of faith. The children of Israel carried with them the coffin of a national savior and the coffer of the covenant, showing a belief that could not be cancelled by death. The great missionary Paul said, "In everything, being afflicted, but not distressed; perplexed, but not despairing; persecuted, but not forsaken; cast down, but not perishing—always carrying about in the body the deadening of Jesus, that the life of Jesus may be manifested in our body. For we who are living are ever being given up to death because of Jesus, that the life of Jesus may be manifested in our mortal flesh" (2 Cor. 4:8-11). By faith we carry the death and resurrection of Christ with us as the enabling power to live in assurance of God's promises. Death demands despair and surrender, but we meet it with faith and perseverance.

The Faith of Jesus Christ

In Galatians 3:23-25 Paul made a strong and peculiar statement. Paul called the coming of Jesus Christ "the coming of faith." Certainly there was faith before Christ came in the flesh. Hebrews 11 makes it abundantly clear that many have lived and died in faith. Yet, by expressing his thoughts this way, Paul helps us realize that the faith of Jesus Christ was of a monumentally different purity and composition than our faith. Christ's faith was so far superior that the display of His faith may be spoken of as "the coming of faith."

Furthermore, the display of the faith of Jesus Christ became the pivotal point for a change in the way God deals with mankind in the accomplishment of His purpose. Christ's faith is indivisibly linked with the revelation of the Son of God, which is also the revelation of God as Father. Now in grace we are living by faith which is of the Son of God (Gal. 2:20). No longer are there legal requirements for a relationship to God by covenant, but we are graced to become His sons (Gal. 4:1-7).

How was this great faith displayed? Certainly, in all that Christ did and said throughout His life, He displayed His faith. Yet there was one pivotal event that sorely tested the metal of His faith to reveal any possible flaw. This testing occurred in Gethsemane and on the cross. People today struggle endlessly, worrying that something they have done places them beyond the reach of God's acceptance. But on Jesus Christ was laid the sin of the whole world (Jn. 1:29), not simply the sin of a single life. He was made to be sin "for our sakes that we may be becoming God's righteousness in Him" (2 Cor. 5:21). And when the sin of the world had settled down upon Him, and when God had forsaken Him in the darkness, He faced death. He faced the end of His existence! Unless the God Who had made Him sin for our sakes, and unless the God Who forsook Him in the darkness chose to raise Him back to life, His existence would cease eternally.

Christ so thoroughly realized the character and purpose and power and love of His God and Father, that, even after His unfathomable separation from God on the cross, His faith still claimed, "Father, into Thy hands am I committing My spirit" (Lk. 23:46). In speaking these words, Christ was quoting Psalm 31:5, and He stopped in the middle of the verse. He could not yet speak the next line with His lips, but without a doubt, He was shouting the next line from the bottom of His heart: "You have ransomed me, O Yahweh, El of faithfulness!" At the moment of His death, this was Christ's thought and faith.

If we believe death is a blissful condition enjoyed in the presence of God, we will fail to grasp the magnitude of the faith and sacrifice of Christ. Furthermore, we will fail to grasp the importance of faith in our own lives. Faith and expectation in Christ's return, and our resurrection at His command, are the indestructible strands, fashioned from the faithfulness of God, which secure us in the heart of oblivion and transport us to the crystal pavement upon which the throne of God is founded.

Conclusion on the First Death

The dead are oblivious to any feeling, either pleasant or painful. There is no consciousness or awareness of the passing of time or of anything in death. Other than relief from the struggle and release from a mortal body, there is no benefit in dying for those who have run their race. Death provides them nothing. Death is the enemy that tears us from the land of the living, grieving our loved ones. Apart from the resurrection, death would be the end of our existence.

And yet, it is good that God has designed death this way. Death is a means of accumulating humanity so that it may step forward in huge grandiose strides in God's purpose. Many, many generations of believers will be raised simultaneously and meet the Lord together. Whether they have been in the grave for a day or for a thousand years, to the consciousness of them all, it will seem as if the moment of dying was the same with the moment of rising from death. The delay between each ones' death and Christ's coming will seem nonexistent to all. What a marvelous way to bring all the generations together into the light of life, releasing them from the grip of the enemy.

The resurrection of Christ is monumental! It is the victory in which we will all participate. It is the promise of our own raising. And it is the revelation of the sons of God! As easily as our hands pass through the air, with such ease the powerful hands of the resurrection of Christ will reach into the dust of the earth and raise up the millions of humanity. Adam, Eve, and every last one of their children will see life again, because of the resurrection of Christ Jesus!

Our faith is to be exercised by focusing on Christ. For Him we wait. He alone is our Deliverer. As He died, looking to His Father to bring Him back into existence, so we look to Him as we face death. Our existence, our life, depends upon Him. His return will save us, out of the life of this world, or out of oblivion. Our faith should grapple with that reality.

Preface

In the life of David was typified the grandest conflict and the most exultant victory the universe shall ever witness. In the weakness and simplicity of youth and the power of faith in God, the shepherd boy defeated the veteran warrior, Goliath, beheading the Philistine with his own sword. Some years later David took up that sword again, using it in the establishment of his kingdom (1 Sam. 17:51-54; 21:8-9).

Death, the first death, is a power committed to the Adversary. Death is the sword in Satan's hand by which he enslaves humanity to fear (Heb. 2:14, 15). But on Golgotha (which may have received its name as the place where David placed Goliath's head as a memorial 1 Sam. 17:54), in the weakness of human flesh, and the power of faith in God, Christ crushed the head of the ancient serpent, and since has been nullifying all the Adversary has done (Gen. 3:15; 1 Jn. 3:8).

Now the Lord, Christ, has said, "I have the keys of death and of the unseen [hades]" (Rev. 1:18). No faithful Israelite feared Goliath's sword, when it was held fast in King David's hand. And we need no longer fear death, because Christ has conquered it for us. Death will be under new constraints in the full establishment of our Lord's kingdom. The difference in character of the One Who now holds the sword of death is sufficient reason to put away every fear.

THE SEARCH FOR THE SECOND DEATH

Questions

There are not many passages in the Bible that mention the second death by name. And those naming the second death are not concerned with defining its features. Because of this, many questions regarding the second death arise, questions which can only be answered by a study of many different, but related passages.

It becomes apparent that one great question over all must be answered first, "Is the second death a repetition of the first death, or is it something else?" The answer to this question must be verifiable in every case.

Is the second death the same thing as hell, or hades? Is it the same thing as Gehenna, the same as Tartarus? If it is not the same as one or some of these, how is it different?

Is the second death only mentioned in the book of Revelation? If it is, has too much been made of these comments from a dark and difficult portion of the Bible?

Is the second death literally death—is it the same as the first death? And is the lake of fire literally a lake of fire? In studying the first death, it has been shown that death is a state in which there is no conscious existence. If the lake of fire is literal fire, then the second death must be literal death, since casting a person into fire will kill them. But the passages referring to the second death do not speak of people dying but of torment which continues for extended periods of time. Why do those cast there not quickly die? What keeps them alive? A person will die in a number of days without water. An environment of fire would drastically increase dehydration. What keeps people alive? Are there water fountains in the lake of fire? Literal fire will destroy body tissue. If people are to live for extended periods of time in literal fire, they must be healing as quickly as they are being burned, or else they will quickly die and the lake of fire will, in effect, become an enormous crematorium.

Does literal fire have the capability of tormenting spiritual beings such as Satan? How is he tormented in the lake of fire?

Literal fire also raises questions with time periods. Fire is a chemical reaction in which substances change—fuel is burned and ash, or something which cannot be burned remains. How is the fuel supply maintained? A literal fire large enough to engulf millions of people could be the size of a flaming planet. Will such a spectacle be part of the new earth?

Judgment at the great white throne is according to works, or, acts. No two people are alike. How can people be thrown into a fire and all endure different torment? Are there *hot spots* and *cooler spots* in the fire?

Is the second death a figurative expression? If it is figurative, what does it signify? If the second death is figurative, is the pain and torment real? How are figurative expressions to be understood? Why would God use figurative expressions and not speak plainly about something so serious that will affect so many people?

Who is consigned to the lake of fire? Is it people, spirits, Satan, beasts? If it is people, is it only the most extremely wicked people that are consigned there? If the lake of fire is such a terrible punishment, why are some said to be there during both the thousand years and the age following? Satan is not cast there until the thousand year period is over, and after he leads a great revolt! Is Satan's torment shorter or less severe than that of the ones he deceived?! Why do some others appear to be there longer than he?

The lake of fire is in existence during the thousand years and also in the age following. But the lake of fire is not named the second death until after the millennium, and not until the great white throne judgment is reached. Does the lake of fire change at the time of the great white throne judgment? Is it something different in one age than it is in the other?

Why does the Bible speak of being injured by the second death, but doesn't speak of dying the second death?

Different ages have been mentioned in the questions above. How do they figure into this problem?

We hope to answer these questions, and more, to the reader's satisfaction.

BIBLICAL TIME PERIODS

The Eons of the Eons

In the following pages reference will be made to *the eons of the eons*. The following brief explanation of this term should enhance the reader's understanding of the author's viewpoint. The book of Revelation frequently uses the phrase, *for the ages of the ages*, or, *for the eons of the eons.* Since this phrase defines the time period for torment in the lake of fire, it is essential to understand what it means.

Most English versions erroneously render this phrase *forever and ever.* Rotherham's *Emphasized Bible,* Robert Young's *Young's Literal Translation of the Bible,* and the *Concordant Literal New Testament* are among the more well known versions that use *age* or *eon* rather than *ever.* The *American Standard Version*, (1901 ed.) gives the rendering of ages in the margins.

The Greek word in question is *aion,* and it clearly does not bear the meaning of endlessness. The versions which translate *aion* as *ever,* or, *forever and ever*, also frequently translate this word as *world,* not to mention other less frequent renderings such as *world began, evermore, course, eternal,* and *ages* (these examples are from the AV). The translators were forced to use additional words, such as *world,* because consistent use of *forever* would have resulted in many contradictions. For example, "...the harvest is the end of the *world*" (Matt. 13:39 AV). Consistent translation would have read, "the harvest is the end of *forever*". But *forever* cannot have an end! (Also compare Matthew 13:40, 49; 24:3; 28:20). 1 Corinthians 10:11 mentions, "...the ends of the world (AV)". It is difficult to imagine a world having more than one end, but not only is the word for *end* plural, the word for *world* is plural also. Paul is not speaking there of several worlds ending. He is speaking of the consummations of various ages in God's plan and purpose.

The more recent English versions generally replace the use of *world* for this Greek word with *age*. This may be helpful to understanding individual passages, but the continued use of the term *forever and ever* in other passages precludes understanding of the intended meaning of the Bible in many contexts. The overall impact of such inconsistency is confusion to the serious student. The thoughtful reader should well ask the question, "If forever means endless, then what does forever **and** ever mean?" Endlessness is an adopted idea that is foreign to this word. Consistency in translation will eliminate the words *forever and ever.*

The reason this phrase occurs frequently in Revelation is because that book is primarily concerned with events of the coming ages, and of the events occurring in the eras of the kingdom. Isaiah, Peter and John all saw the new heaven and earth, and understood it to be a part of the kingdom. And so it is. But it occurs in a different eon than the millennium. Many millenarians think of the millennial age as being the final aspect of things before the commencement of a *final state*. It is helpful to realize that the duration of the kingdom spans a period of time that includes an entire eon, and part of the eon before and much of the eon after.

In the impending eon, Christ is figured as the Lion of the tribe of Judah, and it is an eon of strict rule in justice and righteousness. The impending eon includes the millennium. The eon following the millennial eon is the *eon of the eons.* It is the one in which the final stages of God's great plan for creation reach their consummation. In that eon Christ is figured as the Lamb, and reconciliation is the major theme.

The phrase *eons of the eons* applies to the two greatest eons of all the eons. These eons are the impending eon (containing the thousand years, or millennium) and the final eon, (known as the *eon of the eons* Eph. 3:21) the greatest eon of all. The great white throne judgment occurs after the thousand years, but during a portion of the eon containing the thousand years. These two eons are divided by the passing away of the present heaven and earth, and the coming of the new heaven and earth.

This phrase, the eons of the eons, follows a form of Hebrew expression which is used with many words. The King of kings is the greatest king of all kings, having authority over all. The holies of holies (Heb. 9:25) are the two most holy places. They are more holy than any other place inside or outside the camp. They are more holy than the altar and laver and everything in the outer court. The song of songs is the greatest song of all, extolling the merits of love, something that is of far greater value than all of one's possessions, something that is strong as death.

The eons of the eons are the greatest eons of all, because in them God's purpose comes to full fruition. In the eons of the eons the earth will see true justice. In these eons judgment on humanity is completed. In them death becomes limited, and is finally abolished. In these final eons glory to God continually increases. And in these eons the consummation of vivification (when all are made immortal) is reached, and God becomes All in all.

Kingdom Eras

Grasping the scope of the kingdom may be easier when considering it from the viewpoint of three different eras. The kingdom can easily be divided into three eras which all occur in different eons, simply by noting the presence or absence of Christ and Satan. The first era occurs in the present eon. It is outlined in the parable of the wheat and tares (Matt. 13:24-30, 36-43). The householder who sowed good seed is the Son of Man, Christ. The field is the world. The tares, or darnel, are the sons of the wicked one. The tares are sown among the good seed by the Adversary, Satan. This shows the Adversary still to be at large in the world during this era of the kingdom. Other parables indicate an absence of the householder after the sowing of the seed (cf. Matt. 25:1-30; the delayed bridegroom and the traveling lord of the slaves. See also Lk. 19:11-27). This era of the kingdom closes an eon, because Christ said the harvest at which the tares and wheat are separated was the conclusion of the eon (Matt. 13:39 not the end of the world or the end of forever). This harvest judgment cannot be the same as the great white throne judgment and the lake of fire, because Satan was present during the preceding time.

During the following eon Satan will be absent from world affairs for a thousand years, because he will be locked up in the "bottomless pit," or, "submerged chaos" (Rev. 20:1-3). Following the eon containing the thousand years is the eon of the new heaven and earth, when Christ rules as the Lamb on the great white throne with His Father. During that era of the kingdom, Satan is removed from the pit and cast into the lake of fire. Satan is clearly shown to be in three different spheres during these three eras. The locale of Christ's presence may not be as clear, but definite distinctions can be made, both in His bodily presence and in the character of His rule during these eras.

These three eras of the kingdom are parallel to the three periods of David's reign. Each period commenced with an anointing. The first period began with the anointing by Samuel and was characterized by persecution from Saul. The second period began with the anointing at Hebron over the tribe of Judah. The third began with the anointing at Jerusalem, after Zion finally fell into the hands of Israel.

Eternal or Eonian?

The word *aion*, also has an adjective derived from it: *aionios*. This word is frequently translated *eternal* in the common versions, as in the phrases *life eternal,* and *everlasting punishment* (Matt. 25:46 AV). But the meaning of the adjective does not go beyond the meaning of the noun from which it is derived. Something that is yearly pertains to a year. Something that is monthly pertains to a month. And something that is eonian pertains to an eon. Something that is eternal pertains to eternity, and the concept of eternity is in the scriptures only as a result of inaccurate translation. The eons are the largest time segments discussed in the Bible.

If the saved are raised to *eonian life*, rather than *eternal life*, does this mean that at some future time they could die? No. Paul makes it clear that when the saved are changed they will become immortal (1 Cor. 15:53-54). What then is the significance of the term *eonian life*? This term speaks of the *life of the eons*, and has reference to the kingdom eons. The saved are blest, not only to be recipients of immortality, but also to participate in the kingdom. They will be alive during the kingdom eons and some of them will reign in the kingdom. This is the significance of what is generally called *eternal life*. *Eonian life* is a fuller and richer expression because it carries with it the thoughts of all that will transpire during the kingdom eons, when God's purpose is being completed. *Eternal life* only means *endless life*.

Aion and *Aionios* Twice in One Sentence

"And these shall go away into everlasting punishment; but the righteous into life eternal" (Matt. 25:46 AV). Augustine popularized an argument which is based on this verse, and which was made in support of the opinion that *aionios* meant *endless* or *eternal*. *Aionios* is used twice here in the same sentence, rendered *everlasting* once and *eternal* once. Simply stated, the argument is this: The same word is used to describe the life of the righteous that is used to describe the punishment of the wicked. Therefore, the life of the righteous and the punishment of the wicked must be of equal duration.

Others have come behind Augustine and added teeth to his argument saying that if anyone, man or God, used a word twice in the same sentence, intending that each usage of the word have a different meaning, that individual was treacherous and deceitful. Therefore, since God is good and righteous, God intended the word to have the same meaning in both occurrences. Furthermore, anyone claiming that the punishment of the wicked is not endless is treacherous and deceitful and opposed to the truth, because the life of the saved will surely be endless. This argument has been a well-ridden horse wherever the controversy on these words has been voiced.

In principle Augustine and company are correct. However, they err in taking for granted that *aionios* means *eternal*, and *aion* means *ever. Aion* is an *age*, and *aionios* means *pertaining to an age*. Would that Augustine's party would answer one question: "If a word must retain the same meaning when used twice in the same sentence (and, in this case, we wholeheartedly agree it should), then why is no one fervently condemning the inconsistent translations of these very same words where they are used twice in a sentence in other passages? Consistency in the following passages would lead to correction of the renderings in Matthew 25:46.

Romans 16:25, 26

"Now to him that is of power to stablish you according to my gospel, and the preaching of Jesus Christ, according to the revelation of the mystery, which was kept secret since the *world* [*aionios*] began, but now is made manifest, and by the scriptures of the prophets, according to the commandment of the *everlasting* [*aionios*] God, made known to all nations for the obedience of faith" (AV).

In these verses the word *aionios* is used twice in the same sentence, and neither of the two words used to translate it can be used in both occurrences without turning the sentence into nonsense. If *world* is changed to *everlasting*, or *eternal* for consistency, then there is a secret that is kept secret eternally, but now is made manifest—an obvious contradiction. If *everlasting* is changed to *world* for consistency, then the God of the gospel is the *world God.* But currently Satan is the god of this age and the kingdoms of this world (2 Cor. 4:4).

In truth, the passage speaks of Paul's gospel, which contains secrets hidden during previous eons—"times eonian," which the eonian God has now brought to light. Understanding *aionios* to possess its meaning of *pertaining to an age* or *eon* is the only consistent way to make sense of the passage. And to speak of the eonian God no more limits His existence, than speaking of the *God of Abraham* limits Him to being the God of only one man.

Titus 1:2

"In hope of *eternal* [*aionios*] life, which God, that cannot lie, promised before the *world* [*aionios*] began" (AV). If eternal were the consistent rendering here, God would have promised life before eternity began. No question of the duration of God's existence is intended here, but how can anything be promised prior to a time period which has no beginning? By definition, nothing can be done before eternity.

If both uses of the word were translated *world*, the passage says that before the world began, God promised *world life*. What is that? The animals have *world life*. This expression tells nothing of the life of the saved. God promised eonian life, the special life of the kingdom eons, in Christ, before eonian times. This makes sense, and this is consistent with a meaning that the scriptures clearly attribute to this word.

Galatians 1:4, 5

"Who gave himself for our sins, that he might deliver us from this present evil *world* [*aion*], according to the will of God and our Father, to whom be glory for *ever and ever*.[*aion* /*aion*] Amen" (AV).

Here the double use of the noun in a single sentence is demonstrated, rather than the adjective. With consistent translation and the meaning of *ever*, Christ's saving work was to deliver believers from the present evil forever, or present evil eternity. Will there be no end to evil? On the other hand, what is the meaning of glory to God *for the worlds of the worlds*? Ephesians 3:9-11 gives another sentence with *aion* used twice, and the meanings are rendered differently. And 1 Timothy 6:17-19 provides a sentence in which both *aion* and *aionios* are used with conflicting meanings. The correct translation of these words is critical if one is to grasp the purpose of God in any significant depth. Augustine's argument is built on one verse, while ignoring five others that would have illuminated the error.

Realizing that the eons in God's purpose are not endless will open the door to a greater understanding of that purpose. And consistent translation of these terms will open panoramic new vistas of God's workings. The correct translation of these words will also raze the abusive myth of endless torment for the lost.

The Scope of Salvation

The study of the second death will lead us into the final time periods of the current ages when God's purpose of salvation in Christ is completed. To understand our place in that course of events, we need to realize the purpose of our salvation in the overall view of God's purpose.

The teachings of endless torment and endless separation from God fall with the correct translation of *aion* and *aionios*. Eventually, when God's purpose of the eons is concluded, all will be at peace and unity with God. This raises questions: What, then, is the gospel for? What is the purpose of belief? Why should we try to share our faith with others? Believers today do not possess the only salvation, but they do possess a *special* salvation. "...we rely on the living God, Who is the Saviour of all mankind, especially of believers" (1Tim. 4:10).

When God clothed Adam and Eve in Eden, He made a sacrifice for all humanity. Granted, at that time there were only two, but he included both the deceived and the one that chose to be disobedient. And His promise was that the Seed would inflict a mortal wound on the one that brought about their death. While many details were lacking then, we understand that the Son of God, the Seed, came to annul all the acts of the Adversary (1 Jn. 3:8). This includes the act that brought death to all humanity. Christ will reverse that curse for all.

The theme of deliverance through the promised Seed resurfaced in Abraham. This childless man with a barren wife became a father of nations. His seed would be a blessing to all. His seed would be as the dust of the earth (Gen. 13:16), as the stars of heaven and as the sand on the seashore (Gen. 22:17).

When God made a covenant with Israel at Mt. Sinai, He said they would be "a kingdom of priests, and a holy nation" (Ex. 19:6). It became clear that the Seed through which God would destroy the works of the Adversary would not be limited to the single individual, His Son. There would be more who would serve under the authority of the Son.

When God entrusted a ministry to the apostle Paul, He revealed that in the final time periods of His saving purpose there would be an administration which would bring the entire universe under the Headship of Christ, and that this administration would include both those of the heavens and those on the earth (Eph. 1:9-11). For this reason, the citizenship of the body of Christ is in the heavens (Phil. 3:20, 21). Believers today are being saved to display God's grace and to be part of the administration which will bring the entire universe into subjection and unity under the Headship of Christ. A reborn Israel will carry on this ministry on the earth while the body of Christ is employed in a similar ministry in the heavens. Those saved today have a special salvation, and, in the future it will be realized that it is not the only salvation.

TORMENT

Torment for the Eons of the Eons

Three passages are noted here, and their bearing on the second death must be taken into account.

"If anyone is worshipping the wild beast...he shall be tormented in fire and sulfur...and the fumes of their torment are ascending for the eons of the eons. And they are having no rest day and night..." (Rev. 14:9-11).

Notice that the fumes of their torment ascend. As long as the fumes are ascending, they are being tormented. The phrase, "they are having no rest day and night", makes it clear that the reference is not to fumes that remain long after a conflagration has ended. This torment is current and occurring during at least a portion of both of the final eons.

"And her smoke is ascending for the eons of the eons (Rev. 19:3). As much as she glorifies herself and indulges, so much torment and mourning be giving her....And the kings of the earth, who commit prostitution and indulge with her, will be lamenting and grieving over her whenever they may be observing the smoke of her conflagration, standing afar off because of the fear of her torment..." (Rev. 18:7, 9, 10).

Those who make up the great prostitute endure torment during at least a portion of both of the final eons.

"And the Adversary who is deceiving them was cast into the lake of fire and sulfur, where the wild beast and where the false prophet are also. And they shall be tormented day and night for the eons of the eons" (Rev. 20:10).

According to these passages and their contexts, those worshipping the wild beast and its image, those getting the emblem of the beast, the great prostitute—all the people of whom she consists, the wild beast—all the people of the kingdoms of which it consists, and the false prophet—all the people of whom it consists, are subject to torment during the final two eons. This wording, *for the eons of the eons*, does not require that every individual involved be tormented for the entire duration of both eons. But the words of the Bible do require that the torment of these groups endure for at least a portion of both of the final eons. If the lake of fire, the second death, was literal death—it could hardly be described as torment for the eons of the eons. People cannot live long enough in literal fire to merit a term such as *eons of the eons*, much less, *forever*. And a dead person cannot be tormented. The theories of annihilation and execution in the lake of fire deny the truth taught in the passages above. All of the unbelieving will be alive at some time during the eons of the eons.

Worse even than the teachings of annihilation and execution, the teaching of endless torment in literal fire, has even less foundation. The biblical sense of torment will be examined shortly and found to be something quite different from the widely held view that can hardly be called anything less than torture. The capacity for torment indicates life, and that the second death is not literal death.

Revelation 20:15 stands in notable contrast with the three passages above: "And if anyone was not found written in the scroll of life, he was cast into the lake of fire." This statement is made with reference to the great white throne. The notable feature is that no duration of time is mentioned with regard to those cast into the lake of fire at the great white throne judgment. As it is so consistently present in the other verses, it might be expected that the phrase *for the eon* would be attached here. The absence of the phrase may insinuate that for some at the great white throne the sentence served may be quite brief. Since that judgment relates to all who were not designated before in grace, it is expected that there will be considerable variation in both length and severity of sentences passed there. Also, the great white throne will be judgment for individuals. Where the torment is said to last for long periods of time, it is referring to groups, such as the beast, which is made up of many kingdoms of people.

The Timing of Eonian Torment

The division of the final eons is marked by the passing away of the present heaven and earth in fire. Does the great white throne judgment occur before, during or after this event? John does not go into detail discussing the conflagration, but Peter supplies some details (2 Pet. 3). John's emphasis is on different matters. Three different verses in the Revelation have been connected to the awesome conflagration to come. The first is Revelation 20:9, where fire descends from God and consumes those assembled against the saints. But supporting evidence that this includes the conflagration of the planet is lacking. Besides, the saints are on the earth, surrounded by the murderous assembly. Another verse is 20:11: "And I perceived a great white throne, and Him Who is sitting upon it, from Whose face earth and heaven fled, and no place was found for them." Some have remarked that the fleeing of heaven and earth may refer to the great conflagration. The writer understands this verse to mean the appearing of the throne and the One sitting upon it are so dreadful and awe-inspiring that those of the earth and the spiritual beings of the celestial regions would all vainly seek for a place to hide from the impending judgment.

The final verse is Revelation 21:1. "And I perceived a new heaven and a new earth, for the former heaven and the former earth pass away, and the sea is no more." The writer believes that here John refers to the conflagration of heaven and earth with the simple phrase "pass away". This view is supported by the order in which John relates the vision. Follow the various scenes of the vision, noting the phrase, "And I perceived..." (Rev. 20:4, 11, 12; 21:1, 2). Also notice that in the scene of the great white throne, "the sea gives up the dead in it" (20:13). But, on the new earth, "the sea is no more" (21:1). Evidently the great white throne judgment will occur during the final era of the millennial eon. The judgment must begin while this present earth is standing for the sea to give up the dead that are in it.

There is another comment which insinuates the time of the great conflagration. During this event "earth and the works in it shall be found" (2 Pet. 3:10). This suggests that the conflagration of the earth is itself a judgment upon the works of humanity on this planet. The time of the great white throne judgment is when humanity's acts are judged. It seems fitting that these occur at the same time. Probably it is better said that the conflagration is one aspect of the great white throne judgment.

This order of events dictates understanding the second death as figurative. If the great white throne judgment occurred during the millennial eon, and if the second death were literal death, then all those not receiving life at the great white throne would be dead during the final eon. This would mean that no one would suffer torment or affliction during the final eon, because only the righteous would be alive. Then the scriptures which mention torment for the eons of the eons would be violated.

It might be suggested that this torment during a plural number of eons refers to torment during the climax of the present eon, in the tribulation era, and then during the millennial eon. But that suggestion is preposterous. This current eon is described by the Scriptures as the "present wicked eon" (Gal. 1:4), and an eon of which Satan is god (2 Cor. 4:4). It cannot be viewed as one of the *eons of the eons*. The eons of the eons are the most glorious of all the eons. If the current eon were named one of the eons of the eons, then the basis would be laid for Manasseh to be termed king of kings, the tower of Babel to be termed holy of holies, and apathetic Ecclesiastes to be termed song of songs.

Torment Defined

What is the nature of the torment that will be endured during the eons of the eons? The fire and sulphur suggest that it will be intense and thorough. A perusal of the biblical usage of the word *torment* will be helpful in grasping its scope.

"And they bring to Him all who have an illness, those with various diseases and pressing torments, also demoniacs and epileptics and paralytics, and He cures them" (Matt. 4:24).

"Lord, my boy is prostrate in the house, a paralytic, dreadfully tormented," (Matt. 8:6). [The amount of pain a paralytic could feel is questionable. Probably here the reference is to mental anguish at least as much as to physical.]

"...the ship was in the middle of the sea, and He was alone on the land. And perceiving them tormented in rowing, for the wind was contrary to them..." (Mk. 6:47, 48).

"Now the ship was...being tormented by the billows, for the wind was contrary..." (Matt. 14:24). (Though this usage is obviously figurative, it is still descriptive and helpful.)

"...Lot, harried by the behavior of the dissolute in their wantonness (for the just man dwelling among them, in observing and hearing from day to day, tormented his just soul by their lawless acts)..." (2 Pet. 2:7, 8).

"...Locusts...and license was granted them as the scorpions of the earth have license. And it was granted to them, not that they should be killing them, but that they shall be tormented five months; and their torment is as the torment of a scorpion, whenever it should be striking a man..." (Rev. 9:3, 5).

These examples show torment, not only in the sense of physical pain, but also in conviction of the conscience, mental anguish, frustration, strain, physical exhaustion and depression. All of these aspects of torment are expected to be included in the chastisement upon the unbelieving. In none of these biblical examples do we find literal fire as a source of torment. The proper aspects of torment will make up the chastisement of each individual as he or she grows in subjection to God.

Fumes of Torment

Reference has been made to "fumes of their torment" (Rev. 14:11), and "the smoke of her conflagration" (Rev. 18: 9). There are some interesting parallels to these phrases: "... incenses, which are the prayers of the saints" (Rev. 5:8; see also Rev. 8:3-4), and "Then the priest will cause the whole to fume on the altar. It is an ascent offering, a fire offering of fragrant odor to Yahweh." (Lev. 1:9). The fumes of incense and the smell of meats and juices cooking over the fire would be much more pleasant than the fumes and smoke of torment. Smoke burns the eyes, and fumes given off by torment are not likely to be pleasant (cf. Isa. 65:5). Yet there is a similarity in the description of these things that should not be unnoticed. They all ascend to God, and they come as the result of trials, which are represented by fire. Since they originate in trials, they represent the experiences which are needed to bring about a realization of the truth. This shows the beneficial purpose inherent in all God's judgments, and it shows He takes pleasure in some of His creature's trials while other trials are not pleasant to Him, though needful. This illustration also shows how thoroughly the figurative use of fire permeates the scriptures. It is fully bound up in the primal thought of sacrifice.

Sulphur—Brimstone

The association of sulphur (*brimstone*: Middle English: "to burn + stone") with the lake of fire should not be overlooked. When sulphur is burned, sulfur dioxide is produced. Sulphur dioxide is a nauseating, suffocating gas. The gas is easily liquefied and is used as a bleaching agent and disinfectant, as well as other things.

The gas, sulphur dioxide, is generally present in volcanic eruptions. It was known to the people of biblical times through familiarity with volcanic activity, and it would also be known to the Jewish people through the biblical record of the destruction of Sodom and Gomorrah. Since sulphur is mentioned in connection with fire, it seems likely that the primary significance of the sulphur is to intensify the idea of suffering, misery and discomfort.

Sulphur was used in the ceremonial purifications of false worship in ancient times. There seems to have been considerable knowledge of its properties. This is not to suggest that something additional to the cross is needed, but to explain the figure. The cleansing would be for those whose place is in the fire, and not for the cleansing of the earth from them. The new earth is brought about independently of their cleansing. The ideas of stifling volcanic fumes that would take away one's breath, coupled with the idea of cleansing, suggests a kind of suffering that would make one weary of the flesh and all its desires.

Was the Cross Enough?

The lake of fire is the sentence passed at the great white throne judgment. Some who understand the second death to be literal death would have the sentence from the great white throne served at the throne before the individual is executed in the lake of fire. But if the lake of fire is understood figuratively, it can indeed be a condition in which the judged live under various degrees of servitude and hardship. The judgment will be suited to each individual, because it is made according to their acts.

Some argue against the second death being figurative, saying it suggests a means of salvation other than the sufferings of Christ. Such a thought is immeasurably removed from the writer's intent. Call to remembrance that it is graciously granted to believers to suffer for Christ's sake (Phil. 1:29). Paul suffered intensely (Phil. 1:30; 2 Cor. 11:21-33), and even spoke of his sufferings as "filling up...in His [Christ's] stead, the deficiencies of the afflictions of Christ" for the sake of the ecclesia (Col. 1:24). Paul adamantly declares that believers are "complete in Him" (Col. 2:10). Yet he also speaks of participating in Christ's sufferings, conforming to Christ's death, and of being a libation—a complementary gift—added to the work of Christ (Phil. 3:10; 2 Tim. 4:6; Phil. 2:17). The work of Christ on the cross has removed the offense and distance from God toward man. But that is not the limit of God's workings in His purpose to become All in all. Judgment is still needed to remove the enmities and wounds between man and man, between man and self, and from man toward God. When God's plan is accomplished, man will be at peace with God, at peace with his fellow man, and at peace with himself. The judgment at the great white throne is designed to finish this work. Truly this great and feared judgment is a work of mercy and grace by our loving Father. It will bring so many to completion.

Possibly all this is best understood in the light of 1 Timothy 2:4: "God,..wills that all mankind be saved and come into a realization of the truth." Christ is a correspondent Ransom for all (1 Tim. 2:6). Therefore nothing is lacking in His sacrifice to save all. Yet the additional purpose of God's will is that all come into a realization of the truth. God has determined that realization is to be gained by means of experience and suffering. We believe that Christ was a perfect man, yet we read of His being perfected through His sufferings (Heb. 5:8, 9). This perfection then, was not the correction of any flaw, but it was the perfection of completion that comes with realization. In taking on humanity, Christ's realization of mankind's frail condition and needs was completed. Likewise, we may be saved, but even while we are saved we fall short of what we must become. A believer's salvation can be expressed as the Lordship of Christ in their life. Yet, throughout his lifetime the believer comes to realize new areas of his life that must be submitted to Christ. The believer's subjection to Christ is not instantaneously complete. It grows and develops with the believer. And so it is with those of the second death. Their ransom has been paid in full, but God will not be satisfied until they come to a realization of the truth to enable them to embrace God and love Him and be one with Him.

The greater one's realization of the truth, the greater also is the truth's impact on their life. If those in the second death are in a living, mortal condition, their experiences and sufferings will have a cleansing effect on their conduct, provided those experiences and sufferings bring them to a greater realization of the truth. This provides explanation of what we are intended to understand by the figures of fire and sulphur.

Death: The Teacher

"And instructing is Yahweh Elohim the human, saying, 'From every tree of the garden, you are to eat, yea, eat. Yet from the tree of the knowledge of good and evil, you are not to be eating from it, for in the day you eat from it, to die shall you be dying'...

"And unclosing are their eyes, they two, and knowing are they that they are naked. And sewing are they fig leaves and making for themselves girdle skirts" (Gen. 2:16, 17; 3:7).

Death was the consequence of disobedience to God's instruction (Rom. 5:12). It was not immediate death, but mortality, which would result in death. What is meant by the *unclosing* or *opening* of the eyes? Remembering that this was a tree of knowledge, closed eyes would be figurative for ignorance. Adam and Eve could certainly see things around them, and Adam's naming of the animals pre-supposes intelligence and perception, but in the arena of good and evil they were ignorant and unskilled. The opening of their eyes was a realization of their need of righteousness and of their offensiveness to God because of their disobedience.

Since God is operating all according to the counsel of His will, the outcome of this seeming tragedy will certainly highlight His beneficent purpose. Apart from the knowledge of good and evil, man has no love of the truth, no awe of the glorious perfection of God, and no appreciation for his situation, no matter how pleasant. With the knowledge of evil and realization of offending God, man is being prepared for a realization of the love that overcomes all evil and forgives every offense. Death, though strict and ruthless, is an excellent teacher, and it is, in the long run, beneficial to man.

Death's didactic method has two aspects. First of these is in the process of mortality. The daily, devitalizing effects of death divest mankind of all confidence in the flesh. The second aspect, dying, looms up continually before man, intimidating him and reminding him of his weakness. What greater incentive could man have to turn to God? It could hardly be thought strange that the second death would also have such a teaching ministry.

And if the condition of mortality and the realization of death are divinely appointed teachers, may not those who have never had opportunity to contemplate those lessons yet be taught by them? It is not the unsaved who occupy the mind here, but those who die as infants. God could judge them at the great white throne, return them to the grave (if that were the second death) and raise them at the consummation. But how are those who have never lived to be judged? What is to be judged? What acts or deeds have they committed which qualify them for judgment? It is irrelevant to say their *sinful nature* or the *latent sin* within them is judged. The Bible clearly says that the great white throne judgment is according to works or acts—sin is not the issue. On what grounds would God's judgment be based? What realization of good and evil do they possess which could give them an appreciation of righteousness and holiness and love?

Here are two untenable suppositions: (1) that God can judge the deeds and acts of those who have never consciously done anything; (2) that such a judgment could prepare individuals for the appreciation of truth, love, righteousness, holiness, or any other virtue. Such a course is foreign to God's method and purpose. Was the very purpose of Eden not to teach humanity of its needs by the experience of good and evil, and to ultimately be blessed thereby? God's will includes both salvation **and** realization of the truth (1 Tim. 2:3-6). It is apparent that God intends this realization to be the result of the experiences of mortality and of His judgments.

Those whose eyes never beheld the light outside the womb still have much to learn. It is often asked if those who died as infants will be raised as infants or adults. We know of no place where the scriptures answer that question. But there is no apparent need for the infants to be raised as infants rather than adults. The world is even now filled with adults who have yet to learn the lessons of childhood. The real issue is not the physical maturity of those dying as infants. The issue is whether God will supernaturally endow millions with a realization of the truth, or if they will experience things of consequence themselves. If the former of these two methods were employed, one is left pondering why humanity and the spiritual realm were not endowed with this realization at the time of their creation. If creation is benefited through the long and tedious presence of evil, why should this large segment of humanity be deprived of its benefit? These thoughts again support the view that the second death is figurative. It is a living condition of mortality in which humanity learns many valuable lessons, at and after the great white throne judgment.

If the objection is raised: "Death is an enemy! How can such an important teaching ministry be accredited to an enemy of humanity?" We reply that death is also a judgment of God. "The judgments of Yahweh are truth; they are righteous altogether; coveted more than gold, and more than much glittering gold, and sweeter than honey and drips of the combs. Moreover, Your servant is being warned by them;" (Ps. 19:9-11). The cursing of the ground that accompanied death, and all the trials that follow with it are for humanity's sake (Gen.3:17).

FIRE: LITERAL OR FIGURATIVE

Because the lake of fire is definitive of the second death, the nature of the lake of fire must be determined. The lake of fire is known prior to the great white throne judgment, being extant throughout the thousand years. Yet the lake of fire is not called "the second death" until the time of the great white throne judgment. Does the great white throne judgment cause a change in the lake of fire? What will the lake of fire be during the millennium? A brief overview of the use of fire throughout the scriptures will provide a basis for understanding what is meant in these final pages of the book.

Literal Fire

Fire is mentioned in the Scriptures in a wide variety of usage. Literal fire has issued forth at different times in extraordinary fashion. Fire and sulfur rained down on Sodom and Gomorrah (Gen. 19:24; Lk. 17:29). Aaron's sons, Nadab and Abihu were consumed by fire when fuming incense with "alien fire" (Lev. 10:2). At Israel's complaining, the fire of Yahweh consumed many on the outskirts of the camp (Num. 11:1, 2); fire from Yahweh consumed 250 people in Korah's rebellion (Num. 16:35; Ps. 106:18). Obviously literal fire kills. Fire fell from heaven: on Elijah's sacrifice and altar (1 Ki. 1:9-15); on the altar of David at Ornan's threshing floor (1 Chron. 21:26); upon the sacrifice at Solomon's dedication of the temple (2 Chron. 7:1-3); and upon Job's sheep and shepherds (Job 1:16). There are other instances when it is insinuated that God issued fire, particularly on sacrifices. Also, there are many occurrences of the word fire where it refers to the fire upon an altar of sacrifice or the fire that accompanied the sacking of a city. There is little, if any, controversy over such passages, but considerable confusion remains where fire is used as a descriptive term when referring to divine judgments.

Figurative Fire

The Bible frequently mentions fire in relationship to God. The messenger of Yahweh appeared in the burning bush (Ex. 3:2), but, since the bush was not consumed by the fire, apparently the heat associated with literal fire was absent. The pillar of fire by night marked God's presence and protection over Israel, and the presence and leadership of His messenger (Ex. 13:21, 22; 14:19,24; 23:20; 40:38; Num. 9:15, 16; 14:14; Deut. 1:3; Neh. 9:12, 19; Ps. 105:39; 121:6). Because of these many references, it is not surprising the author of Hebrews wrote, "...our God is a consuming fire" (Heb. 12:29). Is fire that changes to cloud, and then changes back to fire the same literal fire we know, or are we meant to understand things about God that may be represented by the characteristics of fire? Even though these two examples were visible to humans as literal fire, certain characteristics of fire appear to have been suspended, raising questions regarding its literal reality.

In Deuteronomy 9:3 Moses said that Yahweh was going before Israel, exterminating the Canaanites like a consuming fire. But the books of Joshua and Judges record no such fire, if it must be understood literally. In Judges 9 fire from Abimelech and fire from the men of Shechem was to consume each other. The fire from Abimelech was his military campaigns against Shechem. The fire from the men of Shechem materialized in a piece of millstone, thrown from a window in the city wall by a woman, mortally injuring Abimelech. Perhaps this fire is best understood as the heat of their anger. In Isaiah 19:19-21 people are described as fuel for the fire, but the context shows the fire to be a civil war.

Isaiah 30:30-33 is a good example of the use of multiple poetic figures employed for emphasis. In addition to the "blaze of a devouring fire", Yahweh's voice and arm and turbulent anger are part of the artillery. He uses a club and a rod and He comes with a crash and storm and heavy hail. Further, it is as if an enormous quantity of wood has been amassed for the cremation of the Assyrian army, and it is ignited by the breath of Yahweh which is like a "watercourse of sulfur" (CV), or, "stream of brimstone" (AV). But in 2 Kings 19:35 where the details of this event are recorded, this vast destruction is attributed to the messenger of Yahweh. And the army was not consumed by fire, because the morning light displayed the dead bodies of 185,000 Assyrian soldiers. There was no literal fire. Poetic language such as this enables one to better grasp the emotion and glory of the situation, but it is not intended as a literal description.

In Isaiah 47:14 the astrologers and seers of Babylon are as straw to be consumed by the fire. In Jeremiah 15:14 the fire that would burn upon Israel was the Babylonian captivity. Also in Jeremiah, military overthrows of Moab, Ammon and Syria are referred to as fire (48:44-46; 49:2, 27). In Lamentations 4:11 the fire which Yahweh kindled in Zion which devoured its foundations was the destruction by Babylon. And the fire which devoured the king of Tyre was also the Babylonian army (Eze. 28:18; Zech. 9:4).

In Joel 1:19, 20 the fire is the heat and drought accompanying a locust plague. In Joel 2:3, 5 the locust plague itself is described as fire, since both consume everything in their paths, leaving nothing but bare stalks.

Malachi 3:2-4 speaks of the sons of Levi passing through the refiner's fire to be cleansed so they might acceptably offer sacrifice to God. This echoes the statute of the law that was given for cleansing—all metal implements were to "pass through fire". Utensils that could not withstand the flame were to be cleansed "by the water of impurity" (Num. 31:20-23). Probably this passage was in the back of Paul's mind when he spoke of purging and purifying oneself in order to be a utensil for honor (2 Tim. 2:20, 21). The purging and purifying processes have always been closely related to fire. It is notable that those who believe in torment in literal fire for the lost often use many of the figurative passages above to support their position, but, at the same time they understand passages that speak of the chosen, like Malachi 3, figuratively.

The Greek Scriptures also exhibit similar figurative uses of fire. In Matthew and Luke a baptism of fire, a severe and trying judgment, is said to precede entrance to the kingdom. Those who are not termed "grain" to be garnered into the barn [kingdom] are termed "chaff," and they receive a severe sentence of judgment—are burned up—with "unquenchable fire". The chaff represents the unbelieving Jews who do not enter into any of the kingdom blessings, but are left outside with the unbelieving nations. The chaff Jews are no more cast into literal fire than the grain Jews are piled up in a literal barn, and eaten during the winter, or buried alive as seed in the spring.

Fire is also said to burn up the unacceptable works of believers (1 Cor. 3). There is no need to ask how literal fire might burn up the deeds of one's life. It is obvious the passage refers to the discarding of everything that is unsuitable for reward in judgment, not to literal flames.

KINGDOM FIRE

There are various expressions about fire that relate to the eras of the kingdom. There is gehenna fire, parabolic fire—such as the "furnace of fire", the eonian fire associated with the glory throne judgment, and the lake of fire. And all of these expressions find their fulfillment, at least in part, before the time of the great white throne judgment. Each is worthy of separate consideration, and each needs to have separate and specific definition.

The Fiery Hell

Where did the fiery hell come from? How did it originate? It is the product of inconsistent translation. The translation of the Bible into a language becomes the foundation for the ideas making up a *theology* in that language. When the second death was given a prominent place in defining the first death, and when the word for *grave*, the word for *the place where the bodies of executed criminals were cremated,* and the word for *the place of confinement of spiritual beings* were all translated by the same word, *hell*, the English speaking world was provided with the building blocks of the doctrine of a fiery hell. The following paragraphs strive to provide brief but biblical definitions for these critical terms.

Hades

Hades is generally considered to be the Greek, or New Testament, equivalent of *sheol*, which is the Hebrew, or Old Testament, word that is translated as *hell* or *grave*. Both of these words are rendered as *hell* and *grave*. *Hades* is a compound of "not" and "to see." It is the *unseen*. The Middle English word from which *hell* is derived means "to cover, or, conceal" as the dead are covered in the grave (Oxford Concise Dictionary of English Etymology © 2003, Oxford University Press). To *helle* potatoes was to put them in a pit in the ground for storage and to prevent freezing. To *helle* a house was to cover it with siding. Grave is the better rendering of both hades and sheol. There is no fire associated with the Middle English *helle*.

Two key differences are apparent between what the Bible says about hades and the lake of fire. First, hades is used with reference to those who are dead. But it is the living who are cast into the lake of fire. Second, those cast into the lake of fire experience torment. But the study of the first death has shown that those who are dead are not conscious of anything, and thus are incapable of being tormented.

Fire is associated with hades and sheol, but only in figurative or parabolic contexts. The parable of the rich man and Lazarus is the prime example of this in the Greek scriptures. The song of Moses is a prime example in the Hebrew writings (Deut.32:22), and it should be studied as a parallel passage with the parable in Luke. Literal fire is not associated with hades or sheol.

Gehenna

The *valley of Hinnom*, or *gehenna*, just outside of Jerusalem, is the place where the bodies of executed criminals will be cremated in public disgrace during the kingdom. "And it shall come to pass that, from one new moon to another, and from one sabbath to another, shall all flesh come to worship before me, saith the Lord. And they shall go forth, and look upon the carcasses of the men that have transgressed against me; for their worm shall not die neither shall their fire be quenched; and they shall be an abhorrence unto all flesh" (Isa. 66:23, 24 AV). The fire in Gehenna is clearly literal. Christ gave extensive warning regarding it in Matthew 5, describing the fire and worms that exist there for the consumption of dead bodies. But no one is cast into Gehenna until they are dead. The wild beast and false prophet are cast into the lake of fire "living", and they remain alive there, being tormented the duration of their confinement (Rev. 19:20; 20:10). There is no torment in Gehenna. These differences are too great for the lake of fire and Gehenna to be understood as different terms for the same thing.

Associated with Gehenna is the "unextinguished fire where their worm is not deceasing and the fire is not going out" (Mk. 9:44, 46, 48). Here some have thought to find proof of endless torment, but have only found unexplainable contradictions. The fires are kept burning to cleanse the area of the rotting corpses of executed criminals. The worms are not fire-proof worms with eternal life. They are simply a seemingly endless reproduction of maggots. This means that the fire is not so intense that flies cannot light, lay eggs, hatch young and continue their life cycle. Gehenna is a literal garbage dump, with literal dead bodies, literal fire, and literal flies and maggots. It was a horrible disgrace to the Jews for a body not to be buried, but to be treated as garbage.

Tartarus

Tartarus is mentioned in 2 Peter 2:4 as a place of confinement for angels or messengers that have sinned. No fire is mentioned in connection with Tartarus. The confinement there is said to be in "chains of darkness, to be reserved unto judgment" (AV). There is no reason to identify Tartarus with the lake of fire and the second death. It is only mentioned here because it is also translated as *hell* in some English translations. The variation of words rendered hell is a witness to the liberties exercised by many translators, and the lack of understanding surrounding this topic.

Eonian Fire and the Glory Throne Judgment

The glory throne judgment described in Matthew 25:31-46 initiates the thousand year era of the kingdom by designating the level of privilege or chastening to be enjoyed or endured by the various nations. It should be noted this is a judgment of nations as nations and not of individuals (v. 31). As the basis for judgment is the treatment of the Lord's brethren, the Jews, during the previous eras, it is clear that this judgment is distinct from the great white throne. This judgment appears to be a worldwide correction of the nations for the anti-Semitism of the past two millennia. Israel, in unbelief and Providential design, functioned as priest, slaying the sacrificial Lamb for the sins of the world. The great white throne judgment is concerned with the works and deeds of individuals, rather than nations.

The judgment of the wicked nations receives two descriptions: (1) "...the fire eonian, made ready for the Adversary and his messengers," (v. 41), and, (2) "chastening eonian" (v. 46). These two descriptions must define one and the same thing. It is clear that this eonian fire cannot be literal fire, else it would consume to ashes those nations placed in it, and no chastening can be inflicted on those who are dead and thus unconscious. Too, it is difficult to perceive how a nation—not only the mass of people but also its whole political system—could be chastened in literal fire. How could there possibly be any justice in such an event? Will all people of a nation be sentenced to identical punishment? The sensible and biblical conclusion is this passage is speaking of literal chastening which is figuratively described as fire.

This chastening will take many forms. The nations will pay tribute to the royal nation Israel. Not only gold and silver will be brought, but also incense, timber, and whatever natural resources the nations may have. The nations will rebuild the cities of Israel, and will be the laborers and servants of the Jews. The Israelites will be a kingdom of priests, ruling over the nations (Isa. 60, 61). Justice will be swift and harsh, with capital punishment inflicted regularly (Zech. 14:16-19; Isa. 66:23, 24; Matt. 5:22). Truly it would be much better to enter into the joyful possession of eonian life in the kingdom, being maimed or lame, than to have wholeness and health but to be subject to harsh rule and judgments and to lose the blessings (Matt. 5:29, 30; 18:1-9; Mk. 9:42-48). The nations could not fulfill the many prophetic passages which speak of their servitude in the kingdom, if they were confined to burning torment in literal fire.

The Furnace of Fire

The Bible supplies a number of examples where expressions like "furnace of fire" are used. The bondage of Israel during their sojourn in Egypt is one such example. Egypt is referred to as an iron crucible (CV, "furnace" in the AV; Deut 4:20; I Ki. 8:51; Jer. 11:4). Israel's sufferings were actually for her benefit, "Behold, I have refined thee, but not with silver; I have chosen thee in the furnace of affliction" (Isa. 48:10 AV). The *fire* of the furnace was actually the slavery of Egypt's brickyard.

The Lord's parables furnish a couple more examples of this term: the dragnet, and the parable of the tares (Matt. 13:24-30, 36-43; 47-51). The good are gathered into the kingdom, while the wicked are cast into the furnace of fire. This is not a sentence of capital punishment, those cast into the furnace wail and gnash their teeth. This reaction suggests anguish and suffering as well as remorse. It suggests a keen awareness of what might have been had they been faithful and righteous.

There is nothing about the references to a furnace of fire which suggest literal fire. Since this is the case, it is likely that the furnace of fire is either the same or at least similar to the eonian fire of the glory throne judgment. Eonian fire is literally a chastening, this furnace is literally a chastening and loss, as well as being a condition in which mental anguish and remorse are acute.

The Lake of Fire

The closing chapters of the Revelation (19-22) show the lake of fire to be in existence during both the thousand years and also during the age following, the eon of the eons, when the new heaven and earth come into existence. The duration of the lake of fire clearly refutes any attempt to associate it with the conflagration of the present heaven and earth. The beast and false prophet are cast into the lake of fire when Satan is imprisoned for the thousand years (19:20-20:3). After the end of the thousand years Satan is cast into the lake of fire (20:10); and, from the great white throne, a portion of humanity is cast into the lake of fire (20:11-15; 21:8; 22:14,

15). The lake of fire is not termed "the second death" until the time of the great white throne judgment.

Since the lake of fire is extant during the thousand years, Scriptures that deal with judgments during the kingdom eras—particularly those judgments which are described as fire—may shed light on the lake of fire. Three such groups of passages have been mentioned previously: (1) gehenna fire; (2) eonian fire—chastening—in connection with the glory throne judgment; (3) the furnace of fire. Gehenna fire is clearly distinct from the lake of fire, because gehenna fire is for the consumption of dead bodies, while the lake of fire is a condition in which beings are consciously tormented. The lake of fire, then, has common ground with both the furnace of fire and eonian fire. All three occur during the eras of the kingdom, and all three are conditions of affliction. Unless some clear distinctions can be presented to give these three fiery descriptions separate identities, it would be most natural to assume that they are all descriptions of the same thing. This is especially likely because the groups consigned to these fiery conditions are basically the same. They are the opposers of Christ and His kingdom.

IDENTITIES

Defining the identities of the characters in John's vision is vital to understanding what the lake of fire and the second death are. If the beast and false prophet are human beings, then the lake of fire must be figurative. Humans could not be "tormented day and night for the eons of the eons" (Rev. 20:10) in literal fire. Literal fire would cause death, and then torment would end, long before any period of time approaching *the eons of the eons* could pass. It has been suggested by some that the beast and false prophet are *superhuman*. The term *superhuman* begs for more explicit definition. If it means two humans possessed by evil spirits, the problem remains that the human bodies would be consumed by fire. Perhaps the term means these beings are strictly spiritual. This raises further questions. Is it even possible for spiritual beings to be tormented by literal fire?

Spiritual Beings and Fire

The messenger of Yahweh was seen by Moses as a flame in a bush. Moses was attracted to this spectacle because the bush was not consumed by the flame. The messenger of Yahweh had apparently assumed the form of a flame of fire. The angel of the Lord who led the Israelites through the wilderness was seen as a pillar of fire every night. The messenger to Samson's parents ascended into heaven in the flame on the altar. God's messenger walked with Shadrach, Meshach and Abednego in the furnace, protecting them from the heat. Also, spiritual messengers are called "flames of fire" (Ps. 104:4; Heb. 1:7). There is absolutely no implication these spiritual beings were experiencing torment when they appeared at these times in fire. The false prophet has power to use and control fire, calling it down from heaven into the earth (Rev. 13:13). In Revelation 19:7, the angel who calls the birds of the heavens to the great feast is said to be standing "in the sun". Perhaps those who insist on a literal lake of fire, would care to explain how, in the same vision, the angel could literally be standing in the sun. And if this spiritual being can literally stand in the sun without torment, we cannot imagine any fire kindled on earth that would torment the beast and false prophet, if they also are spiritual beings.

While these passages may not be deemed proof positive that spirits cannot be tormented by literal fire, they certainly raise significant doubt. So much so, that the burden for proof lies upon those who would insist spiritual beings can indeed be tormented in literal fire. In fact, the spirits seem rather to have a great dread of being confined to water (Lk. 8:31; see also Rev. 20:1-3), a substance quite different from fire. The bondage of spirits is apparently more intensive in the darkness of gloom than it is in the burning brightness of fire (2 Pet. 2:4; Jude 6).

A second question to be asked regarding spiritual beings and the lake of fire is this: Can spiritual beings die? If the second death is literal death, would it not be reasonable to assume that it is death for all who are cast there? When the Sadducees questioned Christ regarding the resurrection, Christ said, "For neither can they still be dying, for they are equal to messengers, and are the sons of God, being sons of the resurrection (Lk. 20:36). Christ was "made some bit inferior to messengers,...so that, in the grace of God, He should be tasting death for the sake of everyone" (Heb. 2:9). These passages show that spiritual beings, such as messengers (angels in the AV), cannot die. The lake of fire, then, cannot be death to them. This raises doubt whether or not the lake of fire could actually be literal death for anyone.

Still another question must be considered. If the beast and false prophet are spiritual beings, why are they cast into the lake of fire while Satan is confined to the submerged chaos, or, abyss? Why are they segregated? Why are there two different kinds of confinement for beings of the same nature, if, indeed, they are the same? Or, do the seven headed beast and the false prophet beast represent beings much different from him who is represented by the dragon?

The Adversary and His Messengers

After the great climactic battle of the tribulation era, the wild beast and false prophet are cast into the lake of fire burning with sulfur (Rev. 19:20). This is, evidently, the same lake of fire into which the Adversary will be cast after his thousand year incarceration in the submerged chaos. Here is the question: Are the Adversary and his messengers, for whom eonian fire is prepared according to Matthew 25, the same as Satan and his messengers, who are all consigned to the lake of fire in the closing chapters of Revelation (Rev. 12:7-10; 20:10)?

If the context for determining the identity of the Adversary and his messengers is limited to Matthew 25:31-46, where nations are being judged, an argument can be made for defining the identity in question as an adversarial nation and its emissaries. However, the question then arises: Why does the King not say, "Go from Me, you cursed, into the fire eonian ***made ready for you***?" It seems clear that the context is introducing additional characters at this point—Satan and his messengers.

Also, considering the history of Israel, there has been a considerable number of adversarial nations. Anti-Semitism has flourished around the globe. If adversarial nation were the intended interpretation, the term *adversary* should be plural. Even in the tribulation, it is not a single nation that persecutes the Jews, but rather a global confederation.

When the context is broadened to include the whole book of Matthew, Satan becomes the prime candidate for the adversary mentioned. The kingdoms of the world, which have been persecuting the Jews, are under his authority (Matt. 4:8, 9; Lk. 4:6). The wild beast is described in Revelation as having seven heads and ten horns (13:1), a description which matches that of the great dragon in heaven (12:3) who is the Adversary and Satan (12:6). The political system that will be persecuting the saints during the tribulation is the embodiment of the spiritual powers warring in the celestial realm. Obviously there is no substantial reason for thinking that the Adversary and his messengers mentioned in Matthew 25, who will go into eonian fire, are any different from Satan and his messengers (Rev. 12:7-10) who will be cast into the lake of fire. And since the eonian fire is not real fire, but rather a description of chastisement (cf. vv. 41, 46), the lake of fire also is not literal fire, but a condition of chastisement. The eonian fire, the lake of fire, was prepared for those who are not harmed by literal fire. Certainly the lake of fire is not meant to be understood literally.

The Wild Beast

The Greek word *theerion* occurs more than thirty-five times in the book of Revelation, and it is translated *wild beast* in the Concordant Version. The first occurrence is in Revelation 6:8 and refers to non-domestic animals of the earth, predators in particular. All other uses of this word in Revelation refer to two wild beasts which are not real animals, but are figurative characters in John's vision. In Revelation 13:11 a wild beast comes up out of the land. After its introduction there, this beast is referred to as the *false prophet*. All other occurrences of *wild beast* refer to the wild beast that came up out of the sea (Rev. 13:1).

There is also mention of a scarlet wild beast upon which the great prostitute was seated (Rev. 17:3, 4). Apparently this is another description of the wild beast which came up out of the sea, because it too has seven heads and ten horns (cf. vv. 3, 7). The mention of color does not appear to be a distinction sufficient enough to assume this is a different creature. Similarly, the dragon is called the *red dragon* only once.

The similarity of the wild beast to the beasts of Daniel's vision is so striking it hardly needs to be pointed out (compare Dan. 7:3-7 and Rev. 13:1-2). Like the beasts of Daniel, this wild beast is a political system of power (Dan. 7:17). In Daniel's vision various traits characterize the beasts, representing different kingdoms that arise over the course of time.

When the Adversary is cast down into the earth, his time is short. All aspects of his rule are combined into one beast. All aspects of his rule are in full display at once. His work in the current eon is preparatory for these events.

The wild beast is said to ascend out of the submerged chaos, or, abyss (11:7), and later is seen rising up out of the sea (13:1). The sea is typical of the nations: "These waters which you perceived, where the prostitute is sitting, are peoples and throngs and nations and languages" (Rev. 17:15). This description of the beast identifies it as the Adversary's rule embodied by human governments. This wild beast has ten horns with ten diadems and seven heads, and it receives authority over every tribe and people and language and nation (13:7). "The seven heads are seven mountains where the woman is sitting on them and they are seven kings.... And the ten horns...are ten kings....These have one opinion, and they are giving their power and authority to the wild beast....And the ten horns...give their kingdom to the wild beast" (17:9-17). There is no mistaking that the wild beast is a political system of worldwide power. It is a confederation of kingdoms, and is allied with a religious-commercial system.

In Revelation 17:8-11 the term *wild beast* may appear to be applied to the individual king who wields the power of the beast. However, it would be a mistake to make the beast an individual from this point forward, and then also, on that foundation to say the beast is an individual anti-christ. David is said to have built Zion from Millo, round about and inward (2 Sam. 5:9). But this does not mean that David performed any of the labor of building. The actions of a king are carried out by the kingdom.

In Revelation 17:8 the context returns us to chapter 13 where the beast ascends out of the sea, or submerged chaos. It appears that the time when the beast is submerged in the sea is a time when the *mountain-kingdom* is not dominant.

When it comes to power, its king is the focal figure for the beast. But that does not mean that the king, rather than the kingdom, is the beast. If it were the purpose to speak of the king individually, he would not be referred to as a beast. Beasts are used in the visions to represent dominant kingdoms. This subject will be treated further when we consider *The Interpretation of Visions*.

The False Prophet

The word *pseudo-prophet*, or *false prophet* occurs three times in Revelation. In Revelation 19:20 it is shown to be an appellation for the wild beast that came up out of the land. The term false prophet is descriptive of the character of its office, and it also distinguishes this beast from the wild beast which came up out of the sea. Since this actor in the vision is introduced as a beast (13:11-17), it is also expected to be a system of authority or political organization of some kind. Since it has two horns, and horns usually represent kings, there will probably be a duality in its leadership.

Notice the things accomplished by the second wild beast: it enforces the worship of the first wild beast throughout the earth (13:12), and it causes all, small and great, rich and poor, slave and free, to receive the mark of the first wild beast on their right hand or forehead. By means of this marking it regulates commerce on a global scale (13:16, 17). While the false prophet exhibits supernatural characteristics, it seems reasonable that most of its feats will be accomplished and enforced by some sort of Gestapo-like police force.

Entertain the question again, "Why are the wild beast and false prophet segregated from Satan during the thousand years? Why do they receive different types of confinement?" If it is remembered that the beast and false prophet are systems involving masses of humanity, the answer is obvious. They are different. They are different kinds of beings, and they are on different plateaus in God's purpose. God's purpose is that humanity be freed from the influence of Satan for a thousand years. During the millennial era the political rulers of this world will be sons of the resurrection, filled with the Spirit of God. There will be no corruption in politics. Justice will be meted out swiftly and accurately. Mankind's excuse that things would be better if only man could have good government and be freed from the corruption of dishonesty and vice in leadership will be tested. But after a thousand years of ideal government, Satan will be loosed, and the mass of humanity will be quickly whipped into a frenzy of rebellion against God. The wild beast and false prophet are segregated from Satan because they are composed of humans, not spirits.

The Great Prostitute

Standing in sharp contrast to the Bride, the New Jerusalem, is "Babylon the Great, the mother of prostitutes and the abominations of the earth" (Rev. 17:5). This woman rides upon the wild beast, described as "scarlet…replete with names of blasphemy, and having seven heads and ten horns" (Rev. 17:4; 12:3; 13:1; etc.). The prostitute sits upon many waters, which are "peoples and throngs and nations and languages" (Rev. 17:1, 15). The prostitute is said to be a city, Babylon (Rev. 18:10), which is located where the seven heads, or seven kings of the wild beast are seated (Rev. 17:9). She makes the merchants, the traffickers or *Canaanites*, rich. Their wares include everything from gold, silver and precious stones to grain, livestock, and even human souls (Rev. 18:11-13). As the new Jerusalem, the bride, is the capital of God's kingdom, the great prostitute is the capital of the beast empire.

The prostitute has worldwide influence in commerce and religion. The fate that befalls her is representative of what befalls the entire system, and, to some degree, all those who are a part of that system. While there will be the structure of a city, the city is the people.

Satan

Many students of the scriptures would be surprised by the statement: "John did not see Satan in his vision of the Revelation." John mentions Satan more than once. But the statement is still true. John saw a dragon with seven heads and ten horns. And sometimes John saw the dragon as a serpent, or spoke of the dragon as a serpent (Rev. 12:15-16). John identifies the dragon as Satan for his readers (Rev. 12:9; 20:2). If John had seen Satan as an individual, spiritual being, he could simply have referred to him as Satan. But, by identifying the dragon as Satan, it is clear that John only saw the dragon in his vision, and that the identification was intended to clarify who the dragon represented for John's readers.

This raises an important question: "Why was Satan presented as the dragon?" The similarities between the wild beast that came up out of the sea and the dragon are obvious. Both have seven heads and ten horns. The heads and horns of the wild beast represent kings and kingdoms in humanity. Is it not likely that there is a similar representation in the spiritual realm by the figure of the dragon? The figure of the dragon may include all the spiritual beings who are part of the Adversary's structure of authority.

If the forgoing supposition is true, then the incarceration of the dragon in the submerged chaos also includes the confinement of all evil spirits for that period of time. Where will all the demons be during the time of Satan's imprisonment? Will only the material realm of Satan's kingdom be restrained and not the spiritual realm also?

The term *Satan,* which means *an adversary,* has sometimes been used as a generic term for evil spirits: "And if the Satan is casting out the Satan, he is parted against himself. How, then, shall his kingdom stand?" (Matt. 12:26). This statement was made by Christ, in response to the accusation that He was casting out demons by Beezeboul, the chief of the demons. It is most reasonable that all evil spirits will be restrained during the thousand year period.

In Mark 5:1-13, a man is said to be possessed of an unclean spirit. Inquiring of his name, it became evident that the man was possessed by a legion of demons. In Luke's account this legion requested that they not be consigned to the submerged chaos (Lk. 8:31). In Matthew's account the legion asked if Christ had come to torment them "before the season" (Matt. 8:29). This indicates that they have an expectation of such incarceration, and they clearly fear an impending time of torment. It is not unlikely that the demonic forces empowering the beast and false prophet would go to the submerged chaos with Satan, while all the humans who make up the beast systems would go to eonian chastening, figuratively termed the lake of fire.

THE INTERPRETATION OF VISIONS

The larger part of the book of Revelation is the recording of visions seen by John. The things John saw in the visions represented actual events, but this does not mean that the things he saw were actually the events that would transpire. John's visions were filled with representative characters. Who are the actors in the visions? There are beasts, the woman who gave birth to the male child, the great prostitute, the red dragon, the bride, riders on horses, powerful angels, and others. John adds explanatory comments, showing that many of the actors in the vision represent large groups of people. This is what helps us identify the actors and understand the vision. When some calamity befalls one of the actors in the vision, it must be understood that all those individuals who will make up what the figurative actor represents are affected by the calamity. But the way in which individuals are affected need not be identical to the calamity as it is described in the vision.

The Interpretation of Daniel's Vision

The example of another vision may clarify this point, and it will help to show how inconsistent the interpretation of John's vision has been. In a vision, Daniel saw a beast which resembled a bear. This beast was told to devour much flesh (Dan. 7:5). This beast is often understood to be a representation of the Medo-Persian empire, and is noted as such in some study Bibles. (There are differing interpretations given, and the purpose here is not to endorse any particular view. We are only presenting a common, widely accepted interpretation as an example.) The devouring of much flesh was fulfilled by the spread of this empire through its military and political campaigns. The passage neither says nor implies that anyone was actually eaten by a bear. There were three ribs in the bear's mouth. These have been interpreted as representing the kingdoms of Lydia, Babylonia and Egypt, which the Medes and Persians conquered. But, again, no one in Lydia, Babylonia or Egypt is believed to have been eaten by a bear to fulfill this vision. Neither did a swarm of bears, covering the landscape, move through these kingdoms eating everyone, enabling the Medes and Persians to come in and possess the land. Please bear with us, though this certainly seems ridiculous. Daniel saw a bear with meat in its mouth. This vision was fulfilled by military conquests.

In another vision (chapter 8), Daniel saw a goat trample a ram. This represented the Grecian Empire defeating the Medo-Persian Empire:

> "The ram which thou sawest, having two horns, these are the kings of Media and Persia. And the rough goat is the king of Grecia [Greece], and the great horn that is between his eyes is the first king. Now that being broken, whereas four stood up for it, four kingdoms shall stand up out of the nation, but not in its power" (Dan. 8:20-22 AV).

No one expects for a moment this passage will be interpreted to mean a ram was actually trampled to death by a goat. Nor does this vision mean any people were trampled to death by goats when Alexander led the Greeks to victory over the Medes and Persians. This was a symbolic vision. Daniel is the only one who ever saw the fight between the goat and ram. Daniel is the only one who saw the lion with eagles' wings, the bear with ribs in its mouth, the four-headed leopard with four wings or the diverse beast with ten horns. The people who lived during the times when this vision was fulfilled did not see any of these beasts. They saw the kingdoms and the military and political campaigns of which the beasts were figures.

Notice the quotation from Daniel says, "the rough goat is the king of Greece." Here the king is mentioned as representing the kingdom. This is obvious, since the context goes on to say that the goat's horn represents the first king. And when the first horn was broken off and replaced by four horns, it represented the division of the Greek empire into four kingdoms. So also, the king who is leader of the wild beast empire may be referred to and represent the whole beast system.

Comparing Visions

Keeping the interpretation of Daniel's vision in mind, we would like to make some comparisons between it and John's vision. Daniel beheld the four winds of the heaven striving upon the sea (Dan. 7:2, 3), and John beheld the dragon standing on the seashore, evidently exerting its influence or creative powers upon the waters. Apparently this represents spiritual forces moving upon the volatile masses of humanity. Daniel saw four beasts come up out of the sea (Dan. 7:4-7). The beast John saw came up out of the sea and had features of all of Daniel's beasts. There were features of the lion, bear, and leopard, a sum total of seven heads, and there were ten horns (cf. Dan. 7:4-7 with Rev. 13:1,2). Notice also that this beast is in the image of the dragon (cf. Rev. 12:3).

Having noted these similarities in the visions, we would like to consider John's vision recorded in Revelation 19:11-20:3. The first scene of the vision is a description of Christ with the armies of heaven.

Scene of Christ's Appearance

"And I perceived heaven open, and lo! a white horse. And He Who is sitting on it is called 'Faithful and True,' and in righteousness is He judging and battling. Now His eyes are a flame of fire, and on His head are many diadems, having names written of which no one except Himself is aware, and He is clothed in a cloak dipped in blood, and His name is called 'The Word of God.' And the armies in heaven, dressed in cambric, white and clean, followed Him on white horses. And out of His mouth a sharp blade is issuing, that with it He should be smiting the nations. And He will be shepherding them with an iron club. And He is treading the wine trough of the fury of the indignation of God, the Almighty. And on His cloak and on His thigh He has a name written: 'King of kings and Lord of lords" (Rev. 19:11-16).

Christ's eyes are described as "a flame of fire" (v. 12). His cloak is dipped in blood, and a sharp blade is issuing out of His mouth (vv. 13-15). What is meant by the blade issuing from His mouth? Are we to assume that this will be the actual appearance of Christ when He returns? Are we to assume that when Christ was glorified His tongue became a sword!? Certainly not! But what does this mean?

In Acts chapter five is an example of a sword issuing from Peter's mouth, twice. Ananias and Sapphira wanted to enjoy the fellowship and community living of the church, but they also wanted to keep back a nest-egg for themselves. They sold their property and gave a sum to the church, under the guise that the whole amount was given. Actually they kept part back secretly. Peter perceived something was false and asked Ananias about the amount. Ananias confirmed the whole was given. Peter told Ananias that he had not lied to men but to God. Ananias fell down dead. Later Sapphira came in and Peter asked her regarding the amount. She too confirmed the partial gift was the full amount. Peter told her the feet of those who had carried out her dead husband were at the door, and they would carry her out as well. Sapphira fell down dead. There was no visible blade, but Peter's words were lethal to Ananias and Sapphira.

There is also a typical prophecy of this battle in John's vision given in John's account of Christ's life (Jn. 18:1-7). An armed squad, led by Judas, came to apprehend Christ in Gethsemane. He asked them Whom they were seeking. They answered, "Jesus the Nazarene." When Jesus said, "I am He," they all fell down backwards to the ground, as if they had been struck down. This was a typical fulfillment of Psalm 2 and Revelation 19. Isaiah said, "And there shall come forth a rod out of the stem of Jesse, and a Branch shall grow out of his roots...and He shall smite the earth with the rod of His mouth, and with the breath of His lips shall He slay the wicked" (Isa. 11:1-4 AV).

Jesus Christ our Lord stood outside Lazarus' tomb and commanded, "Lazarus! Hither! Out!" (Jn. 11:43). He is the One Who will return with a shout of command to open the graves of those in Christ who have died. And by His word they will be resurrected and made immortal. When John saw Christ in his vision in the first chapter of Revelation, Christ said, "I have the keys of death and of the unseen" (v. 18). To have the keys of something is to have authority over it. Upon His return, Christ will exercise the authority of death. It will be no more difficult for Him to speak a word and whisk away the life of every soldier assembled against Him, than it will be for Him to shout the command that brings His chosen ones to life. There will be no blade flashing and slashing through the hoards of that great army. They will simply fall dead at the command of Christ. The blade issuing from His mouth is figurative, but it is very real.

Are there horses in heaven? The vision is of heaven open and Christ and the hosts of heaven on white horses. How do the horses travel through space? On what do their hooves find traction? After His resurrection, Christ could pass through walls into closed rooms. He could disappear from one location and reappear in another. What need does He have of a horse? John saw white horses in the vision, but we are not meant to understand them literally. They are part of a portrayal of royal military might.

Scene of the Angel in the Sun

"And I perceived another messenger, standing in the sun. And he cries with a loud voice, saying to all the birds which are flying in mid-heaven, 'Hither! Be gathered for the great dinner of God, that you may be eating the flesh of kings, and the flesh of captains, and the flesh of the strong, and the flesh of horses and of those sitting on them, and the flesh of all freemen as well as slaves, and of small and of great'" (Rev. 19:17-18).

Several questions arise here. First, it is frequently believed that Satan and other spiritual beings will be tormented in literal fire. If that is true, why is this messenger, who is standing in the sun, not suffering from the heat?

Second, does he actually speak to the birds? John heard the messenger speak in a human voice. Does this mean that the birds can hear and understand human language and will respond to it? Or, does it mean that birds understand angelic language and John was able to translate it? How could a messenger, standing in the sun, call so loudly that all the birds flying in the heavens around our entire planet, 93 million miles away, could hear him? And how does the sound of his voice travel through space? Sound cannot travel in a vacuum.

One of the most amazing things we witness in this world is the migration of birds. The migration of the birds is not something that simply comes from their desire to have a warmer place to stay in the winter. It is actually necessary for their survival. The birds are first stimulated to begin over-eating, so that they will have fat stores to provide them with energy for this great flight. Birds normally have from 3 to 5% body fat. But they overeat and begin their migrations with 15% or more body fat. Some birds, which must fly over oceans, may actually have 30 to 50% fat by body weight.

Furthermore, their traveling is timed so that they arrive, mate, nest and hatch their young at a time when there is an abundant food supply in the area to which they have migrated. Most birds fly over land, which allows them to make use of thermal updrafts. Land heats up more quickly than large bodies of water, and therefore heats the air above it, causing the air to rise. This supports flight, especially for soaring birds, like eagles and vultures. Many birds also make use of coastal regions with mountain ranges. The thermal up-drafts over the land get an extra boost from the cooler ocean air flowing in which is then warmed and deflected upward by the ascending landscape.

The land of Palestine contains an amazing combination of these features. The Jordan rift valley is one of the hottest places on earth, and is situated with mountains and between the end of the Mediterranean Sea and deserts to the east. This is one of the most heavily traveled migratory paths in the world. This land is the link between Africa to the south and Europe and Asia to the north. It offers an alternative course to crossing the Mediterranean Sea and the deserts of Arabia. It also offers up-drafts and forage along the way.

Ornithologists have conducted experiments, and say it is proven that the stimulus which causes birds to prepare for and make migrations is sunlight. Their brains are sensitive to the number of hours of sunlight in a day. When the time of daylight reaches a certain threshold, they begin the over-eating necessary to prepare them for migration. Is this not an interesting thought, when reading in the scriptures that a messenger, standing in the sun, is responsible for the gathering of innumerable flocks of birds?

When John saw the vision, he saw a messenger, standing in the sun, calling to the birds. Will that be fulfilled literally? Is a literal fulfillment of those words what should be expected? Or may the fulfillment come about because a messenger of God so affects the sunlight coming to earth that it causes thousands and thousands of birds to migrate at such a time that they will arrive at this battlefield when it is covered with corpses? The fact that the messenger was standing in the sun may be a divine hint as to how the miraculous appearance of enormous flocks of birds will come about. John described exactly what he saw, but the fulfillment of his vision does not require the events he saw to transpire literally.

Scene of the Battle

"And I perceived the wild beast and the kings of the earth and their armies, gathered to do battle with Him Who is sitting on the horse and with His army. And the wild beast is arrested, and with it the false prophet who does the signs in its sight, by which he deceives those getting the emblem of the wild beast, and those worshiping its image. Living, the two were cast into the lake of fire burning with sulphur. And the rest were killed with the blade which is coming out of the mouth of Him Who is sitting on the horse. And all the birds are satisfied with their flesh" (Rev. 19:19-21).

The battle scene is surprisingly short in consideration of the chapters previous that have been leading up to this. But chapters 20 and 21 go on to show that this great victory is but another step up in a continuing ascension to a glorious state. This scene is a showcase of the authority of Christ. The arrest and incarceration of the beast and false prophet show that the greatest powers and authorities in all the kingdoms of humanity must bow to Christ. The immediate slaughter of massive armies shows that He indeed possesses the keys of death and hades. The gathering of numberless flocks of birds shows His control over nature and the animal kingdom. And the first 3 verses of chapter 20, the next scene, show power over the Adversary, Satan, and all evil spirits. To understand these things more thoroughly, we need to contemplate what John saw, what the things John saw mean, and what the difference is between what he saw and what will actually happen.

What Did John See?

What did John see? John saw a blade issue forth from the Rider's mouth, which struck the armies, probably with just a single blow, killing them all. He saw an angel standing in the sun, calling birds to gather and consume the flesh of a great slaughter. And he saw a beast with seven heads and ten horns seized and thrown into a lake of fire. Then the other beast, with horns like a lamb's horns and a voice like the dragon's, was seized and thrown into the lake of fire with the first beast. There these two animals writhed in anguish in the flames. Unable to remove themselves from the lake, they remained there during the coming eras of the kingdom. That is what John saw.

The armies died, but the beast and false prophet were cast into the lake of fire living, and they remained alive there. The armies that died were from the nations of the world that were not part of the beast, though they were subject to its influence (Rev. 16:12-16). This explains why they were killed, but the nations that make up the beasts were tormented for long periods of time.

To our knowledge, the apostle John is the only human who has ever seen the lake of fire. And, unless it is in God's purpose for someone else to see this vision, John is the only one who ever will see a literal lake of fire. John saw two strange beasts thrown into the lake. But, again, unless God shows this vision to someone else, no one but John will ever see these beasts. What *will* be seen during the tribulation and the thousand years? Those living then will see a political organization of nations assembled which will seek to exterminate the saints. But it will be a political organization, not a strange looking animal. And what is portrayed by the lake of fire? How is that to be understood?

Consider the vision again. First, there is a description of Christ, but it is figurative and symbolic, not literal. The way in which the armies are slain in the vision is not actually the way they will die when the vision is fulfilled. The description of their death is figurative. John saw many white horses in this vision, he even saw green horses, but they were part of a vision to enable us to picture a great and powerful army with the greatest and most powerful Captain leading them. They are figurative.

And what is meant by the angel standing in the sun (vv. 17, 18)? Is he actually standing in the fire of the sun, and does he actually call to the birds on earth millions of miles away? Or, is the expression figurative? The answer is obvious.

In the first three verses of chapter 20, which are also part of this vision, Satan is seen as a dragon. This also is figurative. The two beasts—the wild beast and the false prophet—are figurative actors in John's vision. They represent nations and multitudes of people. The beasts are figurative, and the lake of fire is most certainly figurative. Its literal fulfillment will be something other than a *lake of fire*. Nearly everything in the entire vision is described figuratively. It is nothing less than incredible that such a large segment of Christianity would pluck the lake of fire from a vision which is so overwhelmingly figurative and maintain with adamancy that it must be literal.

We know of no records from the days of Alexander the Great concerning a four-headed leopard with four wings—that would have been a notable sighting indeed. No one else saw what Daniel saw. When John's vision is fulfilled, no one at this great battle will be trampled by a goat, or eaten by a bear, or thrown into a literal lake of fire. The question to be answered is: "How *will* this figurative vision be fulfilled?" Before that question is answered, objections to the identity of the beasts must be resolved. The resolution of the identities of the beasts in the lake of fire will lead into the definition of the lake of fire.

The Identities in the Lake of Fire

John saw the seven-headed, ten-horned beast, and the beast with horns like a lamb and voice like the dragon's, thrown into a lake of fire. Some may object that the language of Revelation 19:20 sounds as if it is speaking of two individuals rather than two political conglomerates. How is it determined that two individual figureheads are not the ones in view?

Verse 20 says that "the two were cast into the lake of fire." There is nothing here to determine an answer for the question. The words "the two" can just as easily describe two beasts or two individuals.

The context of Revelation 19:11 through 20:3 (and the extended context as well) strongly favors the interpretation of two beasts. The description of Christ is figurative. Satan is seen as the dragon. The beasts are simply much more in character with the context than two individual figureheads. To introduce two literal beings at this point would be inconsistent.

The Wild Beast

The word "living" in verse 20 adds essential information to the context. First, it confirms that the lake of fire is figurative. The armies literally died at the spoken command of the Rider on the white horse. In contrast with this, the beasts not only are cast into the lake of fire, but they continue living there for long periods of time. Potentially, John could have seen the beasts cast into the fire and consumed there by the flames. But these beasts continue in this fire throughout the thousand years, throughout the time of the great white throne judgment and into the age following. This corresponds precisely with what happens to the nations that make up the beast. They are chastised during those periods of time.

Those who worshipped the beast and received its mark are a part of the corporate whole that is the beast. They will be tormented "in fire and sulphur", and, "the fumes of their torment are ascending for the eons of the eons" (Rev. 14:9-11). This is the same description of torment and the same time frame applied to the beast and false prophet. The great prostitute is also a conglomerate of many people. Her torment is described with the same terms of chronology (Rev. 19:3).

The "sheep and goats" passage, Matthew 25:31-46, is one of the most definitive on this subject. In the section on *Identities* it was shown that the "Adversary and his messengers" is a term that refers to "Satan and his messengers." These are cast out of heaven (Rev. 12:7-9) into the earth. Thereupon they took form in the beast and false prophet (Rev. 12:17-13:15). The "eonian fire" of Matthew 25:41 is literally "eonian chastening" (Matt. 25:46). "Chastening" is the preferred and more accurate translation. "Punishment" is a poor rendering of the Greek, (*kolasis*). Since the lake of fire is the "eonian fire" into which the Adversary and his messengers are cast, it stands to reason that it is "the eonian fire made ready" for them (Matt. 25:41). The Matthew passage tells us that nations of people go into this chastisement. The casting of the beast and false prophet into the lake of fire is actually a visionary depiction of the glory throne judgment in Matthew 25.

For all practical purposes, it becomes immaterial whether the beast and false prophet seen in the vision were seen as beasts or individuals. The nations who will make up the political system known as the beast will go into the chastening prepared for Satan, the beast, and the false prophet. We find the political system of the beast in the lake of fire, regardless of how "the two" of Revelation 19:20 is interpreted.

The section on *Identities* also dealt with the question of whether or not it was possible for spiritual beings to be tormented in literal fire. The conclusion of that discussion was "no"—spiritual beings cannot be tormented by literal fire. Some commentators hold that the two individual figureheads of the beast and false prophet are *superhuman*, and can therefore endure the flames. However, the term *superhuman* is left largely undefined. One has said that the performance of miracles and the statement that the beast died and came back to life (Rev. 17:8-11) verifies that it is superhuman. But the apostles and others performed miracles. Lazarus and others were raised from the dead. None of these have been called *superhuman*. The scriptures speak of two kinds of bodies: (1) bodies of flesh, dependent upon this soil and atmosphere, and, (2) bodies celestial (1 Cor. 15:45-49). The body of flesh dies in literal fire, bringing torment quickly to an end. The celestial body cannot be touched by literal fire. The term *superhuman* is only a fabrication used to elude a predicament. It solves nothing. However, the term *superhuman* points a finger at one of the chief causes behind misunderstandings of the lake of fire. People traditionally think of individuals being cast into the lake of fire. The false teaching of torment in literal fire has been around so long that the context of the book is overlooked, and it is forgotten that John was actually seeing figurative representations as he viewed the vision.

"He," Or, "It?"

The strong tendency to understand the beast and false prophet to be individual, personal beings, rather than conglomerate beasts, is subjective interpretation, rather than objective conclusion based on what John has written. Following are four reasons why this interpretive leap is so easily and frequently taken by students of English versions.

(1) John speaks of Antichrist in some of his writings. The Antichrist is usually identified with the "man of lawlessness," "the son of destruction" (2 Thess. 2:3), and identities in Daniel. These personal and human identities have also been identified with the beast and false prophet in Revelation by many commentators. It may well be true that Antichrist is to be identified with the beasts of Revelation. There is no intention here to endorse or discredit any such interpretations. But neither of the beasts should be identified as a single, individual personality. John's view of matters in the vision is on a much broader scope. Individual kings are sometimes mentioned, but only when their actions of leadership characterize the actions of the beast. But the beasts are conglomerate systems which represent peoples and nations as a unit that is dominated by Satan, and John always views them as beasts, not as individual people. The familiarity of the reader with popular views of Antichrist, and the following three reasons make it a simple matter to leap from beast to person without due cause.

(2) To the English mind, **dragons**, **serpents** and wild **beasts** are things. The pronoun that would represent them is neither *he*, nor *she*. The pronoun to represent these creatures is *it*. In the *New American Standard Version*, the antecedent

pronouns for these terms are translated by the pronouns *he, his, him, who, whose, they* and *them*, 76 times in chapters 12-20 in Revelation. The *New International Version* does the same thing 71 times in the same passage of scripture. The *King James Version* does the same thing 67 times in the same passage. Since the beast, the second beast (called the false prophet), and the dragon are designated by masculine personal pronouns some 70 plus times in the scriptures leading up to the lake of fire, is it any wonder the reader loses sight of the vision as John saw it? The *Revised Standard Version* (RSV) consistently refers to the dragon as *he*, etc., but it consistently refers to the beasts as *it*. *Today's English Version* and the *New World Translation* (NWT) tend to follow the approach of the (RSV). The NWT differs in that it also translates the antecedent pronouns for *dragon* with *it* except where the context seems to make it clear that the dragon represents Satan. The *Concordant Version* retains the correct gender of the pronouns as required by the text and acceptable English. However, this too can be misleading.

(3) *False prophet* is an appellation given to the second wild beast of Revelation 13. This term occurs only three times in Revelation, and it is the context of the final occurrence which verifies that the false prophet is the same as the beast from the land (compare Rev. 13:12 & 19:20). The term *pseudo-prophet*, or, false prophet, is masculine in gender. This would make the correct rendering of its pronoun *he,* in English. But the false prophet, in John's vision, is still a beast—an *it*. The reader needs to be aware that *he*, when used of the false prophet, is equivalent to *it* in English, by virtue of the context.

A similar situation occurs with the dragon. John did not see Satan, the Adversary, as a personal being in the vision. He is always seen as a dragon or serpent. That is why John adds the explanatory identification, informing his readers that the dragon he sees in the vision represents Satan (Rev.

12:9; 20:2). But the popular English versions translate the pronoun for dragon as *he* rather than *it*. In Revelation 20:3 *he* and *him* are correctly used where their antecedent is serpent or Adversary or Satan. But even there, it is the dragon which John sees in the vision. Contextually *it* would be less misleading. The average English reader may not be aware of these issues and the subtle influence they have on his thoughts and interpretation of the scriptures.

(4) English has no plural neuter pronoun for the third person. In other words, English has no plural neuter form for *they* or *them*—a plural of *it*. When both beasts are mentioned, the English pronoun used is *they*, or, *them,* simply because there is no other word to use. If English was to refer to both beasts and maintain the correct gender, it would have to say *the beasts*, rather than *they*. And to do so would not be translation.

The False Prophet

"And the wild beast is arrested, and with it *the false prophet who does the signs in its sight, by which he deceives those getting the emblem of the wild beast, and those worshipping its image*. Living, the two were cast into the lake of fire burning with sulphur" (Rev. 19:20). Do we realize the importance of the italicized portion of this verse, and its purpose in the context? What is the image we visualize when reading this description? In Revelation, the term *false prophet* always refers to the second wild beast which came up out of the land (Rev. 13:11). Revelation 19:20 is the only passage that tells us the false prophet and the wild beast which came up out of the land are the same. The first occurrence of the term *false prophet* is in Revelation 16:13. There John beheld the dragon, the wild beast and the false prophet. Coming out of their mouths were unclean spirits. These demonic spirits resembled frogs. Their task was to mobilize the armies of earth against the Rider on the white horse. Thus it is at the command and authority of the dragon, the beast and the false prophet that the armies assemble. Since the scene in chapter nineteen is the great battle when all these armies were gathered, it is proper to recall this scene of the dragon, wild beast and false prophet with frog demons coming out of their mouths, when contemplating their consignment to the lake of fire. The three who are seen calling the armies of earth together in chapter 16 are the same three who are cast into the lake of fire and the submerged chaos in chapters 19 and 20. Realizing this will help provide a correct image in our minds of what John saw.

John identifies the false prophet at the time it is thrown into the lake of fire. The description by which he identifies it is the same description of its actions that was given when it was introduced as a wild beast, coming up out of the land. This confirms that what John perceived in the vision was two wild beasts being thrown into a lake of fire, not two individuals.

What Will Be Seen During the Kingdom Eras?

As noted, only John has seen these wild beasts as beasts. It is possible the image that will be made and worshipped during the tribulation may resemble what John saw (Rev. 13:14-15), but there is no reason to expect that anyone else will ever see these beasts.

Since the lake of fire is figurative, the questions arise: What will be the literal fulfillment of the lake of fire? What will the people alive during those eras see? There are many literal prophecies referring to this time. The sampling which follows is from Isaiah.

"And the sons of foreigners shall build up thy walls, and their kings shall minister unto thee;...Therefore, thy gates shall be open continually; they shall not be shut day nor night, that men may bring unto thee the forces of the nations, and that their kings may be brought. For the nation and kingdom that will not serve thee shall perish; yea, those nations shall be utterly wasted....the sons also of those who afflicted thee shall come bending unto thee, and all they that despised thee shall bow themselves down at the soles of thy feet;...And foreigners shall stand and feed your flocks, and the sons of the alien shall be your plowmen and your vinedressers. But ye shall be named the Priests of the Lord; men shall call you the Ministers of our God; ye shall eat the riches of the nations, and in their glory shall ye boast yourselves" (Isa. 60:10-14; 61:5-6 AV).

Zechariah adds: "And it shall be that whoever will not come up of all the families of the earth unto Jerusalem to worship the King, the Lord of hosts, even upon them shall be no rain" (Zech. 14:17 AV).

During the thousand years, the world will see the nations living in servitude and subjection to a spiritually renewed Israel. The severity of hardship endured by each nation will be according to its judgment at the glory throne (Matt. 25:31-46).

The Iron Furnace and the Lake Of Fire

The subjugation of the nations to Israel will be the literal fulfillment of the lake of fire. This name, the lake of fire, is a fitting designation for the subjection of the nations, when it is compared with the name given to Israel's former slavery. "As for you, Yahweh took you, and He brought you forth from the iron crucible [iron furnace AV], from Egypt, to become His as a people of allotment" (Deut. 4:20 compare 1 Kings 8:51; Jer 11:4; Isa. 48:10 "furnace of affliction"). No one believes that Israel was literally in an iron furnace or crucible in Egypt. The holocaust of World War II was a different case. But "iron crucible" is the term which God used to describe Israel's torment in the brickyards of Egypt. There was no furnace. The bricks were dried in the sun. If "iron furnace" is a suitable term to describe the slavery and affliction of Israel in Egypt, is "lake of fire" too unusual a term to describe the slavery and subjection of the nations during Israel's reign of strict righteousness? Certainly not!

Understanding John's Presentation

To be the recipient of visions through divine revelation is rare. There is no handbook, other than details preserved in the Bible, to aid in the understanding of these visions. Yet some helpful deductions may be made. It appears that John viewed the entire vision before writing anything. For example, the second death is mentioned very early in the book (Rev. 2:11), though it is not seen or mentioned as part of the vision until the 20th chapter. After seeing the vision in its entirety, with divine inspiration and total recall, John wrote what he had seen and been instructed to write. John freely supplies details as the vision progresses, often anticipating things that will be happening later in the vision. The vision is filled with detailed contrasts.

John uses the word *perceive* when he relates the vision. He grasped all these things mentally. His perception was not limited to visual observance only. He also mentions the time elements which involve ages, though his perception of these things may have been completed in days or hours or even moments. This aspect of timing and duration is helpful in determining whether the lake of fire ever changes.

The Vision Continued

At the end of the thousand years, and after the dragon has led the revolt, he is "cast into the lake of fire and sulphur, where the wild beast and where the false prophet are also. And they shall be tormented day and night for the eons of the eons" (Rev. 20:10). This verse shows the spiritual being, Satan, being placed "where the wild beast and where the false prophet are also." The place the beast and false prophet occupied during the millennium is the same place they occupy during the eon following. And it is the same place to which Satan goes—a place in which he too will become subject to Christ and God. Because the place is the same for the beast and false prophet during both eons, the insinuation exists that there is no significant change in the lake of fire at the end of the millennium or during the final eon. At least there is no change in it as relative to the beast, false prophet and Satan. Will there be any mitigation in the lake of fire when it is designated *the second death* at the great white throne? That will depend on the character of rule that issues from the great white throne.

THE PUNISHMENTS OF THE PARABLES

During His earthly ministry the Lord spoke a number of parables which pertain to the kingdom. The punishments of the parables are grossly misunderstood when they are said to refer to a *hell* with literal fire and unspeakable torment. But to what do they refer?

Hades

Hades occurs as a punishment in the parables only once—in the parable of the rich man and Lazarus. The application that follows from this parable, as mentioned previously, relates to national Israel in the current era suffering the fires of anti-Semitism. There is no fire or literal torment in hades. Christ's portrayal of it in the parable was figurative, to match the death of the rich man and Lazarus, which was also figurative. As the context of Luke's account shows, the rich man and Lazarus both represent large groups of people. It is a nation that dies, not individuals. This parable is different from the others following because it refers to Israel during the interim time before Christ comes. The others relate to the kingdom in its later eras.

Outer Darkness

Outer darkness is the opposite of *inner light*. Is the inner light not that of what Isaiah prophesied? "Arise! Become resplendent! For your light has come, and the glory of Yahweh, it is radiant upon you. For behold, the darkness, it shall cover the earth, and murkiness the folkstems, Yet Yahweh shall be radiant upon you, and His glory, it shall be seen over you. And nations will go to your light, and kings to the brightness of your radiance." (Isa. 60:1-3).

John also spoke of the inner light, saying, "And the nations shall be walking by means of its light, and the kings of the earth are carrying their glory into it. And its portals should under no circumstances be locked by day; for there shall be no night there," (Rev. 21:24, 25).

From these passages it is clear that *outer darkness* (Matt. 8:12; 22:13; 25:30) means being locked outside of the blessedness of the kingdom while others freely enter in. And surely this outer darkness is a condition in which people consciously exist, otherwise their remorse would not be described as "wailing and gnashing of teeth."

Cut Asunder

Cut asunder and appointed his part with the hypocrites (Matt. 24:45-51; Lk. 12:41-46) is another condemnation referring to loss of kingdom privilege. There are numerous passages in the Pentateuch in which a violator of law or someone who had become unclean was to be cut off from the nation of Israel, or cut off from the congregation. In these instances the person was considered an alien and had no part with the nation in their current relationship to Yahweh or in the future kingdom. It does not imply that they were killed. They lost access to the tabernacle, sacrifices and ceremonies of the law. This parabolic phrase is comparable to that condition. The hypocrites are not allowed into the blessedness of kingdom citizenship. They are outside. Those of Israel who are alive during the times of the kingdom, but are not allowed to be citizens of the kingdom, are *cut asunder*.

Wailing and Gnashing of Teeth

Wailing and gnashing of teeth is an expression depicting one who has suffered an inutterable loss. Imagine those Jews who were devout in their religion (but not from the heart) and were expecting their Messiah to come. Generation after generation of Jews had come and gone. Finally the Messiah came but was not recognized. When He returns few will be ready. Think of the feelings of those chosen people, when they stand outside, observing the glorious splendor in which they could have participated. They were always told it would come, and to some degree they believed it. But when it finally came, with glory far surpassing anything they imagined, they found themselves left out. Surely they will wail and gnash their teeth in anguish over their loss.

The Furnace of Fire

The parables of the dragnet and the tares (Matt. 13:24-30, 36-43; 47-51) were mentioned previously under the heading of *Kingdom Fire*. See that section for further details. As with the chastisements listed above, it is a condition of consciousness and chastening.

To Whom Do the Parables Apply?

Do the parables the Lord spoke apply to the people who heard them? Will those unbelieving Jews of the first century be cast into outer darkness, or must these passages only be applied to those living at the time of the Lord's return? In the Revelation we read of only the faithful being raised at the commencement of the thousand years. The unbelieving Jews of past centuries are dead during the millennium. Here is the issue: unbelieving Jews will be raised at the great white throne, but, if the second death were literal death, they would die again without ever seeing the kingdom. So it must be asked, when will they ever witness the kingdom's glory? When will they be cast outside or be cut asunder or wail and gnash their teeth? The parables call for these things to be experienced during the kingdom.

These parables apply *especially* to that generation to whom they were spoken. The only feasible time for that generation to witness the kingdom glory will be following the great white throne judgment. Since they must be alive at that time, the second death must be figurative. Otherwise, the only possible time they could witness any event of the kingdom would be during the time their judgment is pronounced at the throne.

Sentences of judgment are not carried out before the judge's bench, especially if the duration of the sentence spans a considerable portion of time. The second death itself is the sentence of judgment. And if it were not, then why should anyone be cast into it? If the cross has conciliated God to man, and if judgment takes place to correct all the wrongs of one's life, why, after all that is accomplished, should anyone be killed? If the judgment of those at the great white throne was completed there (which it is not), then the only thing remaining for them is to be vivified—made immortal. They would be further advanced in God's purpose for them than believers today who have lived and died. Current day believers are still awaiting judgment after they are raised. The second death must be the sentence issued at the great white throne.

Further light on these thoughts is shone by a passage in Luke where the Lord addresses his comments directly to his listeners:

"Then should ***you*** be beginning to say, '***We*** ate and drank ***in your sight***, and ***in our squares*** you teach!' He also will be declaring: 'I am saying to ***you***, I am not acquainted with ***you***! Whence are ***you***? Withdraw from me, all workers of injustice!'

"There there will be lamentation and gnashing of teeth, *whenever* ***you*** *should be seeing* Abraham and Isaac and Jacob and all the prophets in the kingdom of God, yet ***you*** cast outside. And they will be arriving from east and west and from north and south and will be made to recline in the kingdom of God." (Lk. 13:26b-29).

When will the unbelieving Jews of the first century see Abraham, Isaac and Jacob in the kingdom? They will be dead during the thousand years. Is the era of the second death not the most probable time? Is there any other time they could view kingdom citizens enjoying its benefits while they were left out? And does this not open a window into a broader understanding of the second death? It stands to reason that the expressions, "cut asunder," "cast into outer darkness," "wailing and gnashing of teeth," and other expressions used by Christ in the parables, are all descriptive of the conditions many will enter into after the great white throne judgment. One would expect, then, that such phrases are synonymous with "the second death." And then it would be found that the scriptures actually have a great deal to say about the second death.

THE SECOND DEATH AND ISSUES OF LANGUAGE

Literal Limits and Freedom in Figures

"This is the second death—the lake of fire...the lake burning with fire and sulfur" (Rev. 20:14; 21:8). Here is the inspired definition. A literal interpretation of the lake of fire will correspond with a literal interpretation of the second death. Literal fire kills, resulting in literal death. A figurative interpretation of the lake of fire will correspond with a figurative understanding of the second death. Figurative fire does not kill, and a condition figuratively termed death could be a condition in which torment occurs. Things and experiences may be given figurative names. For example, baby-sitting a spoiled child could be called a *baptism of fire*. But the experience itself cannot be figurative. Whatever is experienced is real and literal, whether the label attached to it is literal or figurative. The torment must be real, but it may be figuratively described as death.

Eonian Life and the Second Death

The Bible never speaks of *eternal life* for believers, despite the frequency of this term in popular versions. It speaks of *eonian life*. Eonian life will be, or become, unending immortality, but the term conveys much richer blessings than simple endlessness or eternality. Eonian life is the "life of the eon", or "life pertaining to an eon." The scriptures, looking forward to the prophesied kingdom, see that kingdom as existing in a distinct age or eon from those of the past. To live in the eon of the kingdom, being a citizen of the kingdom and enjoying all the privileges and blessings of the kingdom, is to have eonian life. Perhaps it was best expressed by the Lord when He said, "I came that they may have eonian life, and have it superabundantly" (Jn.10:10).

The opposite of life is death. For the usual intent, this statement is true enough. It would be difficult to find two other words that express such vivid, deep and meaningful contrasts as life and death. But it needs to be remembered that eonian life is not the only life of the kingdom eons. Multitudes of unbelievers will enter the kingdom eon through the tribulation and still possess the same mortality in which they lived before that phase of the kingdom came. They are not said to have eonian life, even though they will be alive during that eon. All the dead will be raised to life at the great white throne during the kingdom eons, but it is not said that those who are cast into the lake of fire have eonian life, even though they will be alive during the kingdom eons.

Since the life of the faithful in the kingdom is labeled eonian *life*, it would not be an unnatural figure to label the existence of the unbelieving and wicked as *death* of some sort. And since eonian life is not an absolute term (because other life coexists with it), neither must its contrasting figurative term be absolute. Or to put it directly, it is not necessary for the second death to mean death in the absolute and literal sense, particularly since it is applied to those who are not enjoyers of eonian life.

Furthermore, in the context where John defines the second death, it is those who are not written in the scroll of life that are cast into the second death. So the second death is, to some degree, an antithesis to the scroll of life. The contrast makes the name fitting and suitable.

The Power of Figures

"Verily, verily, I am saying to you that he who is hearing My word and believing Him Who sends Me, has life eonian and...has proceeded out of death into life" (Jn. 5:24). We are aware that we have proceeded out of death into life, for we are loving our brethren" (1 Jn. 3:14). The first passage is a quotation from Christ, the second is an application by John. John frequently employs these figurative uses of life and death, and John sets before us the term, the second death.

These passages are only true when understood in their intended sense. The believer has passed the point in life, after which he is sure of enjoying eonian life. But he does not yet experience that life. Even though he experiences a change in attitude, which is reflected in his behavior, he does not yet experience eonian life. Only in spirit, not in fulness, can one experience the life of an eon while that eon is still future. At present only the firstfruits of expectation can be enjoyed. The believers at the time of the Lord's speaking had not yet been resurrected out of death. They had not proceeded out of death in any literal sense. Regarding their future, they had passed the point in their experience when it became sure they would be resurrected from among the dead to enjoy eonian life. Regarding their present life, they had come to the place where their expectation was securely anchored on the promise of what would surely come to pass.

Why do Christ and John employ such language? Death is an unconscious condition—oblivion. In life there is consciousness of self, the environment, emotional, intellectual and moral realms. What two other words could describe such comprehensive contrast? Life and death are basic and familiar to humanity. They provide a powerful and lucid display of the contrast between life with God and life apart from God. Not only is it proper that such a vivid contrast should be employed, but humanity's dulled perception of truth necessitates that the strongest terms possible be used. The power of the figure is justified by the importance of the issue.

Metaphors and the Second Death

"This is the second death—the lake of fire," (Rev. 20:14). This definition of the second death is expressed in the form of a metaphor. A metaphor is a figure of speech in which one thing is said to be another. A metaphor is not intended to be literally true. It is intended to communicate a thought in an effective way by comparing similar features of different things.

Christ said, "I am the Door" (Jn. 10:9). This metaphor vividly communicates the thought that Christ is the way or means by which man enters into life. The thought of this metaphor is lucid, even though the statement is not literally true nor intended to be understood as such. But in the case of the second death, the metaphor is cloudy to many, being shaded by preconceived notions about death, which hinder an objective assessment of the figure.

Metaphors have been at the heart of great controversies. Another metaphor, "This is my body, broken for your sakes," (1 Cor. 11:24), has been misinterpreted to form the basis for transubstantiation. The same, incorrect approach that has fueled bitter controversy over the body of Christ has been applied more widely to the metaphor of the second death to interpret it as eternal death in conscious agony.

Must the Nouns of a Metaphor Be Understood Literally?

E. W. Bullinger, in his renowned work, Figures of Speech Used in The Bible, wrote: "The two nouns [of a metaphor]... are always to be taken in their absolutely literal sense, or else no one can tell what they mean" (p. 736, Baker Book House, 1978). The intent of this statement is clear. It is by the realization of literal things and their characteristics that we have the basis for understanding the figure. Bullinger's remark is a blanket statement that is true in intent and method, but there are cases that take exception to the rule. And even when the nouns are understood literally, the metaphor as a whole is not restricted in meaning to the meanings of the literal nouns. Jesus said to His disciples, "You are the light of the world" (Matt. 5:14). As light brings life and awareness of things to the world, so the disciples, through their conduct and communication bring true life and realization of the truth to the world of humans. But the conduct and communication of the disciples is not literal light.

The metaphor of the second death raises a challenge the definition above cannot meet. Other than the apostle John, not one of humanity has ever seen a literal lake of fire. Not one of humanity has ever witnessed or experienced the second death. Humanity has no experiential knowledge base to understand these terms literally. All that is available for the understanding of these terms is the literal meaning of the nouns and the context of the scriptures. Does this mean the metaphor is beyond comprehension? No.

A writer may not intend the nouns of his metaphors to be understood in "their absolutely literal sense." Figurative expressions may be sufficiently common and well understood to be used in place of a literal expression as part of a metaphor. Does an author not have license to use figurative expressions for one or both of the elements of a metaphor, if he deems such use the most effective means of conveying his thoughts? Is it inconceivable that a writer could use figurative expressions in a metaphor as a means of defining a figure? Granted, the use of figurative ideas in metaphors is less frequent, but the scriptures do provide such examples.

In this metaphor, Christ defined His terms, and then He stated a metaphor which, literally, is a contradiction! "The lamp of the body is your eye. If, then, your eye should be single, your whole body will be luminous. Yet if your eye should be wicked, your whole body will be dark. **If, then, the light that is in you is darkness, how dense is the darkness!**" (Matt. 6:22-23).

Notice especially in this metaphor, "...the light...is darkness," that neither of the nouns should be understood literally. Christ was not speaking of literal light or literal darkness. This metaphor speaks of the contrast between life lived according to a realization of the truth, and life lived according to the desires of the flesh. If both of the nouns of this metaphor were understood in their literal sense, the metaphor would be nonsense.

Notice how John freely amplifies the second element of the following metaphor to further define his figure: "These waters ...are peoples and throngs and nations and languages" (Rev. 17:15). Here is a triple metaphor in which all the nouns are used figuratively: "The seven heads are seven mountains...and they are seven kings" (Rev. 17:9). The seven heads are literally seven heads of a beast which John saw in the vision. Are these seven heads literally seven mountains? And are these seven heads also literally seven kings? Even the kings are not literal. John saw a beast which represented a political system that was a confederation of kingdoms. The kings stand figuratively for their kingdoms. This is a case where three figures are used to explain each other.

Revelation also speaks of two witnesses which are two olive trees and two lampstands, and yet fire issues out of their mouths. Besides this much is said about them which seems to define them as humans (Rev. 11:3-4). The context of the book must be the determining factor for defining such phrases. We cannot rewrite the rules of ancient Hebrew literature to conform to what we might consider correct English.

Discovering the Points of Agreement in Metaphors

The metaphor actually calls for a comparison of similar aspects of the elements of the metaphor. It does not, for even a moment, suggest that the two are identical. Bullinger clarifies further, "The Representation referred to in the figure may not lie upon the surface, and may not be at all apparent in the language itself. It may be in the uses of the thing represented, or in the effects which it produces. In this case the *Metaphor* often comes as a surprise, by the discovery of a point in which two apparently unrelated objects have some point in which they really agree" (p. 736, Bullinger).

The key to understanding the metaphor defining the second death is to discover what aspects of the objects are similar. How is the lake of fire like the second death? At this point the reader does come back to the literal meaning of nouns, even if they are used figuratively, to come to the understanding of the figure as a whole. In this case it is necessary to look for the common thread shared by three literal things: lake, fire and death. The thoughts that come to mind when thinking of a lake are quite different from those associated with fire. But suppose for the moment that fire could be contained in a lake without changing its properties. What are the associations or features of lake and of fire that can remain? By combining lake and fire, many natural thoughts are immediately eliminated. Any thoughts of fish or boats or drinking or refreshment are dismissed.

But other thoughts do remain. Things may be placed or thrown into a fire, or into a lake. And this is a point of agreement required by the context (Rev. 19:20; 20:14). A lake could be a place for washing or cleansing, and fire also is an agent for cleansing. In the law, utensils were to be purified with fire, and those utensils which could not endure fire were to be cleansed with the water of purification. (Num. 31:20-23).

Where, then, is the common ground shared by lake and fire with death? Death is often referred to as a receptacle for humanity. The translation of *sheol* and *hades* as *grave* and sometimes *pit* testifies to this. Like fire, *sheol* is never satisfied, or filled (Prov. 27:20; 30:16; Hab. 2:5). To be placed or thrown into the grave is synonymous with dying. This thought holds the similarity of death to lake and fire.

The association of death with burial also carries the thought of cleansing. Burial allows decomposition to be completed without making the land unclean. Burial brings corruption to an end. Without burial the land is polluted, and stench and disease are rampant. Any contact with a dead person, or even the bone of a dead person made one unclean, and required special cleansing (Num. 19). The Mosaic law even required the burial of human waste (Deut. 23:13), showing burial as a means of cleansing or maintaining cleanliness. As far as the law is concerned, death is the end of sin and its uncleanness (Rom. 6:7 ff.)

And so fire, lake and death all have aspects of agreement as something into which things can be placed or thrown, and as something that has properties of cleansing associated with it. But the scriptures also supply a precedent that is greater than these correlations. Or, perhaps it is better said that the scriptures supply a precedent that is built upon these correlations. That precedent is baptism. There is baptism by water, baptism by fire (figuratively), and burial by baptism into the death of Christ (Rom. 6:4, etc.) These baptisms are all relative to changes in life that are characterized by the death of the flesh and its desires and a newness of life characterized by holiness and spirituality.

All of these baptisms are related to judgments. Water baptism was a figurative judgment on the life of the flesh. Fire baptism was a preparatory judgment for the kingdom. As a burial, baptism shows identity with Christ in His death, which was a judgment on the body of flesh and for sin.

These features of baptisms are what those judged at the great white throne, who enter the second death, need. They will be resurrected for the manifesting and judging of their works. The judging of their works will bring a realization of the truth. This is God's will (1 Tim. 2:4). And the desired result of these things is a renewing of life.

If the objection is raised that these thoughts exchange punishment for renewing, remember that the second death is a judgment of God, and it is for the purpose of setting things right. Remember also that frequently the scriptures are more concerned to express things vividly than to comply with all the specifics of English theological etiquette. Acts 22:16 says, "Rise, be baptized, and bathe off your sins, invoking His name." Anyone who prizes the precious blood and the sufferings of Christ will come to realize that this text is not teaching that washing in water removes the guilt of sins, though many have taught salvation in baptism. Still the scriptures make use of simple, vivid pictures to communicate deep truth.

Part of the reluctance to see these figures for what they are stems from the presupposition that the first death seals the destiny of man. Many refuse to consider that the lake of fire could be a preparation for something else. It is assumed that it must be a final destiny. The failure to realize that judgment is for the purpose of correction is also a hindrance to recognizing God's purpose in the second death. If the wicked were to remain wicked and unbelieving endlessly, there could be no purpose for the great white throne judgment. Why would they be corrected if they and their condition are not to be changed? Unless the condition of those at the great white throne is to be improved, this grand event in the redemptive purpose of God is pointless.

The scriptures maintain that God is in control of all things. This control includes the life situations of the unbelieving and wicked. If judgment is not for their correction and improvement, it could only be to satisfy the wrath of God, Who is ultimately responsible for all aspects of their lives. The thought that God would judge and condemn simply to vent His rage, and without benefiting His creatures, gives a false representation of the God Who is bringing all to a realization of the truth. God has planned a unique path of experience for each individual to travel in coming to realize the truth. This includes the unbelieving as well as those who are given faith.

Parts and Lots

Matthew 24:45-51 and Luke 12:41-46 both relate the parabolic example of faithful and unfaithful slaves. In both passages the unfaithful servant is cut asunder and appointed a *part* among the unfaithful and hypocrites. This is in contrast to being given authority over the household. The word *part* in these passages carries a negative connotation. In Revelation 21:6-8 the same contrast is made. The overcomers enjoy the *allotment* of the water of life and sonship to God, while the others have their *part* in the lake of fire which is the second death. In both cases a division is made. Some receive an *allotment*, others have their *part*. An *allotment*, or, *lot*, was a possession, like a parcel of ground, which was to be tended, worked and enjoyed. It was something from which the tenant of the *lot* was benefited. It is notably different from a *part*. In the parables the unpleasant *part* was to be experienced at the same time as the *allotment* was to be enjoyed. The same holds true with eonian life and the second death.

The Definite Article

Lazarus died twice, but he did not die the second death. He died *a* second death. There are four occurrences of the term, *the second death* (Rev. 2:11; 20:6, 14; 21:8). In each of these occurrences the definite article is part of the term. It is **the** second death, not **a** second death. The definite article signifies that something is distinctive when it is used with *second*. If the definite article were lacking, it would be more likely that the death mentioned should be understood as a repetition or continuation of the first death.

Christ prayed in Gethsemane "**a** second time" (Matt. 26:42). The second prayer was essentially the same as the first. In fact, Mark's account reads: "And again, coming away, He prays, saying the same words" (Mk. 14:39). In Acts 10:13-15 Peter heard a voice "**a** second time." Here the emphasis is not on the actual thought of the words spoken, but simply that the voice which spoke to Peter answered his response.

But, in contrast, a man with two sons spoke "to **the** second" (Matt. 21:30), as distinguished from the first. Joseph was made known to his brothers "in **the** second time" (Acts 7:13) as distinct from the first time that he saw them. The presence of the definite article insinuates that the second death is distinct from the first death. The second death is not identical to the first. Without the article the possibility would exist that the second death could be just *another death* of the same kind.

Outside the City

"And he is saying to me, 'You should not be sealing the sayings of the prophecy of this scroll, for the era is near. Let the injurer injure still; and let the filthy one be filthy still; and let the just one do righteousness still; and let the holy one be hallowed still.'Lo! I am coming swiftly, and My wage is with Me, to pay each one as his work is. I am the Alpha and the Omega, the First and the Last, the Origin and the Consummation. Happy are those who are rinsing their robes, that it will be their license to the log of life, and they may be entering the portals into the city. Outside are curs, and enchanters, and paramours and murderers, and idolaters, and everyone fabricating and fondling falsehood'" (Rev. 22:10-15).

It has been suggested that this listing of sinners outside the city presents the city as a lone island of righteousness in a sea of sin. Further, the solution to this dilemma is to be found in the Greek word *exo*, which is said to mean *left out altogether*, or, *outside in the grave* or *cemetery*, rather than just *outside* the city. This view comes from a confusion of the conditions in the vision with the conditions of John's day.

The Lord's closing words to John here convey a sense of urgency. John's audience is to realize that when the events of this prophecy begin to transpire, they will happen so swiftly that none will find opportunity to make amends or repent for past behavior. The events of the day will whisk them away. Those living in John's day, or any day, were to *rinse their robes* immediately, and live a holy life. Only by doing so could they be sure of having access to the city.

The Greek word *exo* is used at least 8 times to indicate *outside* with reference to a city (Mk. 1:45; 11:19; Lk. 4:29; Acts 7:58; 14:19; 16:13; 21:5; Rev. 22:15). Those who do not rinse their robes are outside. The outside demanded by the context is outside the new Jerusalem. The context reads: "... *entering* the portals *into* the city. *Outside* are curs,..." If those who do not rinse their robes are outside the new Jerusalem, they must be alive on earth during the final eon. This indicates that the second death must be understood figuratively.

Even if the curs, enchanters, paramours, etc., are indeed outside of the city, there is no reason to envision the city as a lone oasis in a wilderness of corruption. Just as those who enter the city are the ones who rinse their robes in John's day, so also, those who are outside the city are termed curs, enchanters, paramours, etc., in John's day. At the time of the new Jerusalem these sinners will have been resurrected, judged, and tremendously enlightened at the great white throne. Furthermore, they will be under the rule of a reborn Israel. It is unthinkable that such dynamic and traumatic experiences as death, resurrection, the great white throne judgment, a new earth, and rule by a vivified, godly nation would have no significant effect on a sinner's behavior. Granted, they are not yet perfected. But man seeks the darkness for the performance of his evil deeds, and the new Jerusalem is a glistening city of light and glory where the darkness of night never falls. From this city fares forth the light of truth that will enlighten and guide the whole world. Furthermore, it is written that "the nations will walk according to this light" (Rev. 21:24). The final age is one in which darkness will decrease as light continually increases.

Injured by the Second Death

The following phrases are descriptive of death as it relates to humanity's experience, and they serve as an example of biblical idiom: (1) "let him decease in death" (Mt. 15:4; Mk. 7:10); (2) "signifying by what death he was about to be dying" (Jn. 12:33; 18:32); (3) "her children shall I be killing with death" (Rev. 2:23). In contrast with these, it is not written that anyone *dies* the second death or is *killed* with the second death. But in a passage where such a phrase could well be employed, something much different is used: "The one who is conquering may under no circumstances *be injured* by the second death" (Rev. 2:11).

The passage does not read: "The one who is conquering may under no circumstances be dying the second death." Neither does it read: "The one who is conquering may under no circumstances be killed by the second death." But if the first and second deaths were identical, such a statement could certainly be used.

The word *injure* in the New Testament is used with reference both to physical wounds (Acts 7:24, 26, 27, etc.), and to the violation of one's rights (Mt. 20:13; Acts 25:10). To suppose that *injure* means *to kill* or *to cause death* is to stretch the word's meaning far beyond its scope. The more viable conclusion is that the second death is figurative while the first death is literal.

THE GREAT WHITE THRONE

The Generations of the Eon of the Eons

"To Him be glory in the ecclesia and in Christ Jesus for all the generations of the eon of the eons! Amen!" (Eph. 3:21) The time period here referred to is the final eon—"the eon of the eons." Who or what are the generations spoken of in the final eon? Is the word *generations* here simply an expression of time? Are these generations the generations of people of past ages? Or, are these generations people who will be born during the final eon? The Scriptures provide limited light, but an opinion will be ventured.

Generation may be used to designate the period of time in which the cycle of human life—birth, growth, maturing and reproduction—takes place. But it is difficult to see how this sense would relate to the rest of the sentence. God will indeed be glorified through the ecclesia and Christ, but this glory will issue from the service for which He has made them competent, not from any physical, developmental changes that take place in them. In the eon of the eons, both Christ and the ecclesia will have long been perfected. And the members of the ecclesia expect to be transformed and receive their perfect, celestial body in an instant, not during a generation of development.

Certainly the glory spoken of here is that ever increasing glory that is associated with the "heading up of all in Christ" (Eph. 1:10). Christ is already the Head of the body, the ecclesia (Col. 1:18). And when the body is glorified with Him, that headship will be complete in the members of the body. But there still remains, in the eon of the eons, multitudes, both on the earth and in the heavens, in whom Christ will be becoming First (Col. 1:18-20). This includes all not yet subject to His Headship at that time.

The context of Ephesians 3 incorporates such thoughts as the evangel of the untraceable riches of Christ, the Father of every kindred in the heavens and on earth, the transcendent love of Christ, becoming completed for the entire complement of God, and the glorification of God through His chosen ones in the culmination of His eonian plan. Bearing these thoughts in mind, it is difficult to think of these generations as being anything other than those still needing their reconciliation to God to be completed during the final eon.

Therefore, it is suggested that the generations of the eon of the eons are the generations of humanity that have been born upon the earth up until the time of the great white throne judgment. There is something very final about that judgment, and it marks a distinct change in God's dealings with humanity. Only one such judgment is revealed in the Scriptures, and it is for the myriad of humanity, except those whom God marked out as recipients of special grace. If more people were to be born during the final eon, it seems likely that another such judgment would await them. We are unaware of any such judgment after the great white throne. Another alternative could be that the judgment of the great white throne would be continuous throughout the final eon until no more of humanity were born and brought to a full realization of the truth in Christ.

The saved who are resurrected no longer marry. The Scriptures do not specifically state the bodily condition of those who are resurrected to the great white throne judgment, though they are certainly not immortal. It is probable that a large number of humanity will come, living, to the great white throne, but the overwhelming majority there will have been resurrected. Is there any basis for thinking that procreation would continue after resurrection?

Man's commission at creation included the populating of the earth. It seems reasonable that this commission will have been completed before the great white throne judgment takes place. Indeed, it seems proper for such a judgment to be waiting for the completion of that commission. From that time forward, the work of reconciliation to God becomes the prime imperative. Each individual that has come into being will come into true knowledge of God.

Of what judgment did Christ speak in the following passages?

"Then He begins to reproach the cities in which most of His powerful deeds occurred, for they do not repent. 'Woe to you, Chorazin! Woe to you, Bethsaida! For if the powerful deeds which are occurring in you occurred in Tyre and Sidon, long ago they would repent, sitting in sackcloth and ashes. Moreover, I am saying to you, for Tyre and Sidon shall it be more tolerable in the day of judging than for you.

"And you, Capernaum! Not to heaven shall you be exalted! To the unseen shall you subside, for, if the powerful deeds which are occurring in you had occurred in Sodom, it might remain unto today. Moreover, I am saying to you that for the land of Sodom shall it be more tolerable in the day of judging than for you." (Matt. 11:20-24)

"Men, Ninevites, will be rising in the judging with this *generation* and will be condemning it, for they repent at the heralding of Jonah, and lo! more than Jonah is here!

"The queen of the south will be roused in the judging with this *generation* and will be condemning it, for she came from the ends of the earth to hear the wisdom of Solomon, and lo! more than Solomon is here!" (Matt. 12:41, 42).

The nations are judged as nations at the glory throne judgment before the millennium, (Matt. 25:31 ff.) but we read of no race-wide resurrection at that time. Since most of those referred to in the passages above are unbelieving, these passages evidently refer to the great white throne judgment.

Some, such as the queen of the south and the repentant Ninevites, had faith. Apparently they will receive life at the great white throne. What of the people of faith from Adam to Abraham who had no expectation of the kingdom? Are they to be incorporated into the body of Christ and raised with them? Possibly, but of the body of Christ it is said that their citizenship is inherent in the heavens. They are designated for a particular location. Neither would those from Adam to Abraham seem to fit into the former resurrection. It seems that if a group of chosen ones lives nearer to the end times, the length of time before their resurrection is decreased dramatically. Also their revelation is more detailed, their selection more specific, their opportunity in the flesh more restricted, and their security more sure. The following outline briefly presents these thoughts.

1. Mankind from Adam: both believing and unbelieving
2. Jews from Abraham: the faithful and obedient
3. The Body of Christ: called out in Paul's ministry

3. Resurrected first to be with Christ in celestial realm
2. Resurrected at beginning of millennium, after tribulation
1. Resurrected at the great white throne judgment

Generation is an outstanding word in the passages above from Matthew. As well as judgment upon an individual's deeds, the scriptures introduce the idea of judgment related to the context of the time and conditions in which one lived. Those with greater light and opportunity are seen as being judged by those who lived in darker circumstances. This is most important to realize, because it clarifies the fact that judgment takes into account every possible influence on the individual's life.

Should not the climactic eon of God's eonian purpose bring special light of the truth to every generation of the various nations? In the word *generation* (Eph. 3:21) is something that is an intrinsic part of everyone's life. Each generation of humanity has its own dreams, problems, hopes and fears. Each generation of humanity experiences its own political, social and economic conditions of blessing, trial or tragedy. And for every generation, the issues of their day make significant impact on their life and actions. Issues confronting some generations are not even dreamed of by other generations.

Shall these innumerable and unutterably diverse aspects of life, which are so indelibly etched in the being and character of all, be nothing more than memories and matters for retrospective discussion after the consummation? Or, shall there be a time when all generations will be convened and made to realize their strengths and shortcomings? Shall there not be a time when all generations will live under knowledge of God, good government, sound economy and proper social standards? Think of what this will mean to the untold generations that have ebbed and flowed with no knowledge of God's love in Christ. If such a time is to come, and it appears that this is a fitting description of the final eon, it will afford every individual the opportunity to grasp the knowledge of both good and evil through their own experience. God will become All in all of all generations.

The Great White Throne

"And I perceived a great white throne, and Him Who is sitting upon it, from Whose face earth and heaven fled, and no place was found for them.

"And I perceived the dead, the great and the small, standing before the throne" (Rev. 20:11, 12a).

With one accord, humanity marches to the grave. With one accord, in ranks that stretch from horizon to horizon, in wealth and squalor, in understanding and ignorance, in hope and despair, in fury and in peace, on bright sunny mornings and in the depths of the night, humanity marches into the dust. But, at the appearance of the great white throne, the dust will give up Adam and every last one of his race. The simple fact that this resurrection will take place is a sign of good things to come.

Along the way a few are given faith, and they rest in the expectation of resurrection to immortality. But why are the rest raised? If, as many creeds affirm, they are not to be the recipients of any blessing, why not leave them sleeping in the dust? What remains to be fulfilled? The souls that have sinned have died (Eze. 18:4, 20; Job 36:14). The law's authority over a man is only for the duration of his life (Rom. 7:1)—it requires nothing more than death. Does the God Who finds no pleasure in the death of the wicked (Eze. 18:32; 33:11) yet desire or require anything other than to have His creation united with Himself?

Those who believe that the lost dead suffer endlessly and consciously from the moment of death, insinuate that a harsh sentence of judgment is already set and in process. This belief requires no resurrection in a body to have a conscious existence. For them the great white throne is redundant, if not senseless and useless. Those who believe in annihilation, if they believe the unsaved are raised, would have them raised from death to be finally and officially executed. This course of events also shows an obvious lack of purpose. If the lost and wicked are to have no part in life from that point on, why resurrect them? If their condition is not to be changed, why judge them? Nay, if their condition is not to be *improved*, why judge them? Is judgment not for the purpose of making things right? Is it right to be at enmity? Is it right to suffer endlessly? Is it right to be tormented without cause?

But worse than the purposelessness of these views are the maligning caricatures they sketch of God. These views escort one within the inner courts of the human temple and reveal there the image of God, graven in the heart and mind by the beliefs and experiences of life. Who is the god worshipped there? Is it the God Who gave His Only-begotten to redeem the world? Or is it one like Moloch, who required the children if the parents were to escape? Or is it one who in insatiable fury would torture the majority of creation in order to allow a few to escape?

The Character of the Judge

God is for order. When the time of the great white throne judgment comes, God's creation will have been chaotic and void of fruit long enough. All is going to be set in order. All is going to be set right. What the character of God is, truly defines what *right* is. And the true character of God has never been more fully revealed than when He gave His Son for all on the cross. At that point God tore open the curtain, as if to say, "Now, for the first time, you are clearly beholding Me. See One Who is bearing the sin and shame of the world, and you are seeing Me!"

It matters not that ten men of different opinion stand with the same Bible in their hands. What matters is the truth which the Bible teaches. What matters are the graces of faith and revelation, and the image of God that realization of the truth carves in hearts and minds.

Resurrection to the great white throne is a siren of grace. Law will have been fulfilled. Sin will have run its course. Good and evil will have been tasted. Indeed, tasted, consumed and digested. But even though humanity's course of humiliation is run, God is not finished with His creation! Resurrection to correction is the rallying trumpet blast of hope and expectation. No matter how severe the needful chastening be (Rom. 2:9), the condition that is extant when God makes things right must be better than the condition previous. The great white throne is a door of love and grace, and the scriptures bear this out.

The Throne

The word *throne* (*thronos* in Greek) occurs more often in the book of Revelation than in all other New Testament books combined. There is reference to the throne of God, the throne of Satan, thrones in heaven and thrones on earth, the throne of the wild beast and the thrones of the saints. The great white throne, mentioned in Revelation 20:11, is distinguished from the thrones of faithful saints, mentioned in verse 4 of the same chapter. It is only called the *great white* throne once, and in following references it is simply called *the* throne, or given other designations.

The appearance of this great white throne in John's vision provides a visible, tangible image to help us grasp the character of the divine authority that is being exercised. It is not a white piece of furniture that is in view. The grand purpose of God is moving forward and great changes are about to take place. The last enemies are being brought into subjection. Instead of rule by the Lion of Judah, the reign of the Lambkin is about to commence. A Lamb that rules! That concept is completely foreign to the thinking of the current age.

A throne is a symbol for authority and power. The book of Revelation shows a great struggle between opposing forces of power and authority, and thus many thrones are mentioned. Typically a throne is a place from which the authority of rule issues forth. A kingdom has only one throne. From this throne decisions issue forth affecting legal, political, military, civil and religious issues. Yet, if many people were asked what the purpose of the great white throne is, the average answer would probably be that it is for the judgment of unbelieving humanity. This answer is only partial. It is quite true that the judgment of the unbelieving of humanity will take place there. But are we to think that once this judgment is pronounced the great white throne disappears or is replaced by another throne? It is not called a *dais*, or judgment seat. It is a throne, and it should not surprise us to find that the scope of its purpose is much broader than judgment.

The Throne Is White

The throne is *white*! By its traditions and claims, humanity has draped the great white throne in the dismal black grave clothes of mourning. They have made it the seat of hopelessness and despair, the seat of fury and incomprehensible woe. But God says that this throne is white. And it is white. It is light, not darkness. White is a color associated with righteousness: "If your sins are coming to be as double dipped scarlet, as snow shall they be white. If they are reddened as crimson, as wool shall they become" (Isa. 1:18 CV). The great prostitute is clothed in cambric and purple and scarlet, but to the bride it is granted to be clothed in clean, resplendent cambric, which is the just awards of the saints. Those who come out of the great tribulation have rinsed their robes and whitened them in the blood of the Lamb, and the armies of heaven are dressed in clean white cambric (Rev. 18:16; 19:8; 7:14; 19:14). "Wash me, and I shall be whiter than snow!" (Ps. 51:7).

The throne is white! All will be set right. The righteousness of God will be served. The issue of all things will be what is right. A simple dependence upon the character of God is sufficient to sweep away all the teachings and theories of humanity. The judgment will not be slack in any detail, but there can be no fear regarding the final outcome.

The Throne Is Great

The throne is great because of the majesty of the One Who is seated upon it. "And I perceived a great white throne, and Him Who is sitting upon it, from Whose face earth and heaven fled, and no place was found for them" (Rev. 20:11). Here sits the glorified Christ, the Son of God. He is described as having eyes like fire and feet like bronze and a voice like many waters and out of His mouth issues a sharp two-edged blade, and His face shines like the sun (Rev. 1:14-16). And He sits on the throne representing His Father, the God of all creation.

Yet it seems that God is seated there as well. God is "the Judge of all" (Heb. 12:23). Along with this thought consider also that "neither is the Father judging anyone, but has given all judging to the Son, that all may be honoring the Son, according as they are honoring the Father" (Jn. 5:22). And yet, just before Christ spoke these words He said, "The Son can not be doing anything of Himself if it is not what He should be observing the Father doing, for whatever He may be doing, this the Son also is doing likewise. For the Father is fond of the Son and is showing Him all that He is doing" (Jn. 5:19-20). Christ expressed this or a similar thought in a very simple manner in Revelation 3:21 when He said, "The one who is conquering, to him will I be granting to be seated with Me on My throne as I, also, conquer, and am seated with My Father on His throne."

Since Revelation 20:11 speaks of the manifest terror of both humanity and the spiritual realm at the appearance of this throne, it is eminently important that we grasp the supremacy of the One sitting on the throne. The unity of the Father and Son is flawless. The Son may be seen on the throne by those who denied and disbelieved and murdered Him. Yet He is there as the representative of His Father, and He may be looked upon as God. However well or poorly we understand these things, one fact remains true. No greater authority exists than that Authority Who will be seated on the throne, and the time will have come for all to give answer to Him. The throne is great because He Who sits upon it is Great.

The throne is great because of the scope of its authority. All those of heaven and earth are convened before it. Never before has the universe witnessed a judgment of such magnitude. Hades will be emptied. All of humanity from Adam forward (except those called before in grace) will be brought to give account. The innumerable throngs of heaven will stand there. The sheer number of beings present there will stagger the mind.

The throne is great because of what it accomplishes. The works of humanity will be judged, corrected, and set right. The minds of humanity will be brought to a greater realization of the truth. The political philosophies and ideals of humanity will be proven. And every religious system will be revealed. All these aspects of human life have parallel aspects to life in the spiritual realm. The spiritual beings will have a similar judgment appropriate for them. In addition, it appears that by this throne comes the judgment by which all the physical works and evidence of humanity on earth, as well those of the spiritual beings in the heavens will pass through the fire. And here is the throne which brings an end to death. This throne is great!

The judgment of this throne is great. We do not know if Adam and Eve lived for days or weeks or years before that one solitary act of disobedience brought the judgment of death upon the whole human race. Some have suggested it was only minutes or hours. Only two out of the billions of humanity were present there, yet all humanity was judged there. When Christ became flesh He underwent a trial by the Adversary in the wilderness. He was on the verge of starvation, and the trials and testing He underwent were much more severe than that of Adam, yet there are many parallels between them. But Christ's testing, and the proving of His faith were not limited to one test in the wilderness. His entire life was a test, consummating in the cross, the most severe trial of all. He proved Himself faithful. His was the second testing of humanity, and He passed the test. And now He is designated by His Father as the Judge. And He Who was faithful through an entire lifetime convenes judgment for all concerning the works and deeds of their lifetimes. And so all humanity that was plunged into a judgment of death for a sin they did not participate in will have a Judge to rectify all the wrongs of their lives, and He is a Judge Who walked where they walked. The throne is great, because of the judgment made there.

The Great White Throne Judgment

"And the scrolls were opened...And the dead were judged by that which is written in the scrolls in accord with their acts...And they were condemned [judged], each in accord with their acts" (Rev. 20:12-13).

The word *condemned,* used here by the CV, comes from a variance in Greek texts. Some manuscripts have *krino*, or, *judged*, and some have *kata-krino*, or, *down-judged,* or *condemned.* Most English translations follow the use of *judged*, rather than *condemned*, favoring judged as the original reading. In the context of Romans 3:1-20, condemned would be in place, but where the context is about to announce the first decree from the great white throne: "...death will be no more…for the former things pass away" (Rev. 21:4) condemnation is out of place.

Acts are the basis of judgment at the great white throne. Notice specifically that there is no mention of judgment according to sins. Sin is directional. It is the missing of His mark, and it was resolved at Golgotha. Deeds and acts are the outworking of beliefs and codes. They are the outworking of character and emotion. They are the embodiment of man's passions. Deeds and acts show us what men's standards are. They show what is inside the human.

The great white throne judgment is the time when every individual, except for those chosen before in grace, will have all of their own personal views, beliefs and understandings brought to the divine touchstone of truth. All that is wrong will become apparent. All that is right will become apparent. The enlightenment shining forth at the great white throne will be of a far greater magnitude than humanity has ever known. The great white throne judgment is illumination, and the sentence that follows is the means of realization.

There has always been light—the light of nature, the light of conscience, the light of the Jewish nation, the light of the church, the brilliant beacon of Golgotha. But all these were lights in the darkness—lights which could be and to some degree have been hidden under bushels. Each human microcosm has had glimmers and rays of illumination. Some have been so enlightened they became luminaries. But the great white throne judgment will be a time when the vast innumerable throngs of beings, both human and spirit, will all be so immeasurably enlightened that it will effect a tremendous illumination of the macrocosm.

In 2 Peter 3:10-13 Peter says that the "earth and the works [Greek: *ergon*] in it shall be found". This happens when the heavens pass by with a booming noise and the elements are dissolved by combustion. Not only are the acts (*ergon*) of one's life judged, but the physical works of humanity will also pass through the fire. The skyscrapers, the bridges, the hydroelectric dams, the landfills brimming with glass, vinyl, newsprint, plastics, disposable diapers and all sorts of the works of humanity shall all be dissolved by combustion. Since this is identified as a judgment upon works it would be appropriate for it to occur in conjunction with the judgment upon the works of peoples' lives.

In fact, this may provide a key for understanding the events of that day more clearly. How are those judged at the great white throne transported to the new earth? This is not so much a problem for those believing that endless, conscious torment in the lake of fire is the judgment pronounced at the great white throne. They usually present the lake of fire removed some distance from the bliss of the new earth. But that view is unscriptural. Those judged at the great white throne will be on the new earth. The leaves of the tree of life are for their healing, not for those who are already immortal. People judged at the great white throne will make up the nations that continue to learn subjection until all are finally headed up in Christ.

The great white throne judgment takes place relative to the present earth. This is apparent since the passage speaks of the sea giving up the dead in it, but on the new earth there is no sea. It seems the judgment transpires on some plane above the earth—a plane of existence maintained by the authority of the throne. If we become captivated by the logistics of these things, we will miss the point. The vision is showing that the entire creation is standing on the ground of judgment, and that the new creation rests upon the just judging of God. While humanity's deeds and works are judged, they will also be witnessing the passing away of earth in fire. All man's works there will be burned. For the celestial beings the same situation is described. They are judged personally, and the heavens, their realm, passes away to be replaced by new.

As all this transpires, there is one great common element that links the new heaven and earth with the old, and that link is this throne. As was noted previously, this throne is called the great white throne only in Revelation 20:11. In verse 12 it is mentioned again, but it is simply called *the throne*. And it must be this same throne which is in view, and from which decrees come forth, while John is beholding the new heaven and earth coming into being, and while the new Jerusalem is descending.

While John is seeing the new Jerusalem descending out of heaven from God, he hears a decree from the throne—what throne? The throne of the context is the great white throne. There is no evidence to support the thought that this might be some different throne which is already in the new Jerusalem as it descends. Instead this throne takes its place in that new city after it comes to earth (Rev. 22:3). And it is by the authority of this throne that humanity is transported from the old earth to the new one.

It was previously noted that the great white throne is shared by the Father and the Son. This agrees with what is found on the new earth. The first two references to this throne on the new earth mention both God and the Son (21:3, 5). And the two remaining references to the throne call it "the throne of God and the Lambkin" (22:1, 3). The writer believes that only one throne is in view from Revelation 20:11 through the end of the book.

So the great white throne is introduced as the seat from which humanity and spirits are judged, and from which the judgment upon this planet and the heavens issues forth. And as these judgments are completed, the first recorded decree from the great white throne issues forth: "Lo! the tabernacle of God is with mankind, and He will be tabernacling with them, and they will be His peoples, and God Himself will be with them. And He will be brushing away every tear from their eyes. And death will be no more, nor mourning, nor clamor, nor misery; they will be no more, for the former things passed away....Lo! New am I making all!" (Rev. 21:3-5). The same great white throne from which all the dead are judged, is the throne which continues on through the final eon and from which the rule that issues forth is described as "a river of water of life, resplendent as crystal." How can the throne from which the decree comes forth: "Death will be no more!" be the bench of execution that so many have made it? This throne has been so little understood.

Death and Hades

"And I perceived the dead, the great and the small, standing before the throne. And scrolls were opened. And another scroll was opened which is the scroll of life. And the dead were judged by that which was written in the scrolls in accord with their acts" (Rev. 20:12).

John's use of the word "dead" here is curious, because he doesn't speak of resurrection until the next verse. There is more than one way in which this is understood. It is not uncommon for John to run with the flow of the vision, and then to back up and give more details. In chapter 21:2 he perceives the new Jerusalem descending out of heaven from God. Later, in verse nine and following he elaborates on the new Jerusalem in great detail. This flashback presentation could be the explanation for John seeing the dead before the resurrection is mentioned. Verses 13-15 would then be explanatory of verse 12.

It is also possible that the word *dead* may be used figuratively here. It could refer to those living on the current earth who go directly to the great white throne judgment without dying first. It may be assumed that those granted eonian life will be all around at the judgment, though they are not judged there themselves. The term could be a figurative antithesis to distinguish between those having eonian life and those who do not.

"And the sea gives up the dead in it, and death and the unseen give up the dead in them. And they were condemned [judged], each in accord with their acts. And death and the unseen were cast into the lake of fire. This is the second death—the lake of fire. And if anyone was not found written in the scroll of life, he was cast into the lake of fire" (Rev. 20:13-15).

The first sentence of this quotation seems redundant. Why is the sea mentioned separately from death and hades? There is a close association of death and hades with thoughts of the grave and entombment. The redundancy of thought may provide emphasis that none are overlooked. None will be left out. Account will be made for Adam, Eve and every last one of their descendents. A lack of proper burial can in no way hamper or limit the power of God to call back all who have died. All life is of the Spirit of God. To think that any of the billions of humanity could be missed or forgotten or overlooked is as unthinkable as accusing God that He could lose part of Himself.

Death and the unseen (hades), as well as the sea, are personified in this sentence. They are spoken of as *giving up their prisoners*. This personification is reminiscent of other passages such as 1 Corinthians 15 where death is referred to as an enemy (v. 26), an enemy which the scriptures taunt as they glory in the resurrection (vv. 54-57). In Romans 6:9 "Death is lording it over Him no longer..." now that Christ is risen.

But the personification of death and hades may aid the understanding of these statements more than would normally be expected from figures of speech. John was beholding a vision. What was he seeing? Death and the Unseen are actors in John's vision that have appeared before. In Revelation 6:8, Death is seen as a rider on a greenish horse who goes about slaying one fourth of humanity. And the Unseen followed him, perhaps as a second rider on another greenish horse—his description is not given. John saw Death, as a Grim Reaper, riding about slaying multitudes of mankind, and the Unseen followed behind collecting the dead.

We are not told exactly what John perceived at this point in the vision, but as we consider the vision in the context of the book, it is not at all unlikely that John beheld two riders on greenish horses cast into a lake of fire. This scenario would be in keeping with the vision as a whole. The important thing to grasp is the literal reality portrayed by the vision.

The casting of death and the unseen into the lake of fire should not be understood as meaning *all those in the realm of death* and *all those in the realm of hades* were cast into the lake of fire. Clearly that is *not* the intended meaning. Death and the unseen had just been emptied by the resurrection to judgment. They are void of humanity when cast into the lake of fire.

The order in which John relates these events of the vision is important, and it raises another question. If the second death were a repetition of the first death, then why are death and the unseen cast into the lake of fire? Instead, we would expect a command to come from the throne:

"Death! Prepare yourself! Prepare to slay the majority of this vast multitude! Fuel the flames of your fires higher than ever before! Hades! Open wide your mouth! Prepare to swallow up millions!" If not this, we would expect John to behold a new rider on a greenish horse, and a new hades following him.

But Death and Hades do not take the roles they have played previously through the ages. A better conclusion is that the casting of death and hades into the lake of fire changes them in some way. Death and the unseen are not living entities to be brought into subjection. Their being cast into the place of subjugation, therefore, must mean that the process and condition of death and hades will be placed under a new measure of control. No longer will death be allowed to run its full course. It will be restricted. This thought is in full agreement with the first recorded decree from the great white throne: "…death will be no more…new am I making all!" (Rev. 21:3-5). The presence of the tree of life and the water of life (Rev. 22:1, 2) ensure that those not yet blessed with immortality will be sustained until the sentence of their judgment is completed and they are vivified. Mortality will continue into the final eon, but it will not be allowed to find its consummation in death.

Cast into the Lake of Fire

"And if anyone was not found written in the scroll of life, he was cast into the lake of fire" (Rev. 20:15).

What is missing here? What might be expected in this verse that does not appear? The advocates of endless torment are quick to add the time duration of verse 10, where the Adversary is cast into the lake of fire, where the beast and false prophet are. "And they shall be tormented day and night for the eons of the eons" (cf. 14:11 & 19:3). The AV inaccurately translates that time as "forever and ever." One reason that time frame is missing is because the first of these two eons is past. The millennial eon closes with the great white throne judgment. But why is there no mention of "torment for the eon," or, "torment for the eon of the eons?" The great white throne brings about a change in the vision. Previously the beast and false prophet, which represent large political systems and groups of humanity were in view. Those beasts, as a collective whole may be seen as being tormented for the eons. But, with the judgment of individuals according to their individual works in view, the length and severity of torment will vary greatly. It is no longer appropriate to speak of their torment in the terms applied to a collective whole.

Just previous to this statement, death and hades were cast into the lake of fire. With that statement, there appears to be a change in death. The second death has been mentioned previously (2:11 & 20:6), but this is the first statement in scripture that provides a definition of the second death and also a reason for the name. This second, race-wide judgment of humanity provides reason for a change in terminology.

The Solution to the Riddle

Several questions cling to the name *Second Death*. Why is the lake of fire *not* called the second death during the thousand years? Why does the lake of fire's name change to the second death at the great white throne judgment? Do any changes take place in the lake of fire that make it different after the great white throne judgment from what it was before? Why is the name *second death* given to the lake of fire? Is that term a suitable name for it?

John saw a lake of fire in his vision—that is the origin of the name. The lake of fire is extant throughout the thousand years, or millennium. During that period of time it is referred to only as the lake of fire, not as the second death. The beasts were cast into the lake of fire at the commencement of the thousand years. The beasts are a figurative representation for the nations of people who were opposed to God and alive on the earth at that time. Any of the people of the beast nations who died remain dead during the thousand years. Therefore, during the thousand years, none of the people of the beast nations living on earth have yet died the first death. This fact makes the term *second death* inappropriate for them during the thousand year period.

A key element of this issue resides with the fact that two distinct time periods in God's purpose are in view. The first is the millennial eon, and the second is the eon of the new heaven and new earth. These two time periods are divided by the great white throne judgment, which comes at the end of the millennial eon. The literal future fulfillment of the lake of fire will be living under some measure of hardship, and learning subjection to Christ. That aspect does not change from one eon to the next. However, there are changes which take place and distinguish these two final eons from each other. (1) The millennial eon will be a time of strict justice, but the final eon will be a time of reconciliation. This is typified by the rule of the Lion versus the rule of the Lamb. (2) During the millennial eon, many in the lake of fire will die, as is evidenced by the presence of gehenna. There the bodies of executed criminals will be disposed. But, during the eon of the new heaven and earth, mortality will not be consummated in death. The lives of all mortals will be sustained by the beneficent rule of their Subjector. "Death will be no more!" (Rev. 21:4). (3) During the millennial eon, the only ones alive on earth who have been resurrected will be God's chosen ones. The thoughts of *second life* and *second death* go together. The chosen ones cannot be harmed by the second death (Rev. 2:11). (4) During the eon of the new heaven and earth, a large percentage of the people on earth will have been resurrected to the great white throne judgment. They will be living a mortal life for the *second* time. This is a significant part of the reason for the term *second death.* Their mortal condition is the final remaining vestige of death on earth.

When Adam was disobedient and sinned, all of humanity was judged under his headship, and the judgment brought death upon all (Rom. 5:12). God's chosen ones are judged a second time, at the dais of Christ (2 Cor. 5:10), under His headship. At the great white throne, the remainder of humanity, who have not yet been judged under the headship of Christ, will be brought to judgment under humanity's new Head. Since the great white throne judgment finishes the *second* race-wide judgment of humanity, the term *second* is especially suitable to the condition which follows. Death was the first judgment passed upon disobedience, shame and unrighteousness in Eden, under Adam's headship. Then it was a mortal condition which consummated in death. Under the headship of Christ, those whose deeds are judged as disobedient, shameful and unrighteous will also live in a mortal condition, but it will not be consummated in death. As they learn subjection to the new Head of humanity, they will be identified with Him in His death and resurrection. Under the headship of Christ, death and condemnation will be abolished and replaced with life's justifying (Rom. 5:18, 19). Ultimately all will be made immortal. Life accompanies submission to Christ's headship. Involved here are some very significant seconds: *second life*, *second judgment* and *second headship*. *Second death* is a natural term to describe the condition of those who are not yet completely released from the dominion of death.

Enemies

Consider for a moment the contents of the lake of fire. It holds the beast, the false prophet, Satan, death and the unseen, and anyone not written in the scroll of life. The first five mentioned are all enemies of humanity. It has been shown that the literal fulfillment of the lake of fire that John saw in the vision will be a condition of subjugation to Christ and His chosen ones. This is what the apostle Paul speaks of in 1 Corinthians 15 when he says that "He must be reigning until He should be placing all His enemies under His feet. The last enemy is being abolished: death" (1 Cor. 15: 25-26). Death and hades are the last of these five enemies cast into the lake of fire. The theme of the subjection of Christ's enemies, quoted from Psalm 110, echoes throughout the New Testament (Matt. 22:44; Mk. 12:36; Lk. 20:43; Acts 2:35; 1 Cor. 15:25; Heb. 1:13; 10:13; and repeatedly throughout Revelation). Obviously the Adversary qualifies as an enemy (Matt. 13:39; Lk. 10:19). Death, the last enemy, is seen in the vision being cast into the lake of fire some time after the Adversary.

Besides these enemies, those of humanity not written in the scroll of life are cast into the lake of fire. There are two criteria mentioned that account for their disposition there: (1) the judgment of their acts, and, (2) their names are not written in the scroll of life. Their acts define a condition of enmity to Christ and the Father. "The disposition of the flesh is enmity to God, for it is not subject to the law of God, neither is it able" (Rom. 8:7). Humanity needs the experiences of evil which are relative to the death of the flesh. By these is the preparation for life in the spirit—life as sons of God (Rom. 8:5-14). The lake of fire will provide the trial needed to burn the disposition of the flesh out of their life, preparing them for the receiving of God's spirit.

As well as being enemies of Christ, everything in the lake of fire may be viewed as an enemy of humanity also. It is easy to see the Adversary and his messengers as enemies. It is also easy to see death and the unseen as enemies of humanity. But how do the faithless of humanity fit such a description? Again, with respect to the lake of fire, it is the acts of humanity—the acts of the flesh—that are in view. Humanity's acts are certainly among humanities enemies. Humanity is controlled by its own actions. How often has one failed to do what should be done because some previous action created prohibitive circumstances? How often does one fail to do what is best, because the actions of another change his disposition? Rather than controlling our actions and doing what is right, our actions and the actions of others, control us. The reign of Christ will end the tyranny of the flesh. From this point of view, we boldly say, the purpose of the lake of fire is to rid humanity of its enemies.

Evidently this is the view that is intended to be taken on this passage. As was noted earlier, there will be some at the great white throne judgment who will receive life. We expect the queen of the south and the repentant Ninevites to be among them (Matt. 12:41-42). They are not numbered among humanity's enemies.

The Glory of the Lake of Fire

The intent of the scriptures is that we should glory in the lake of fire. This statement would probably shock many who hold traditional views. If the lake of fire is seen as a place in which vast numbers of individuals suffer unspeakable torment in literal flames, we cannot glory in it. But, if John's vision is seen for what it is, we may truly rejoice in it. In the vision John was seeing the full and final expression and embodiment of Satan's power and authority in the political and social systems of earth. The lake of fire is where these systems—the incarnation of the Lie—are consumed by the truth of God. The vision shows all Christ's enemies being placed under His feet. The vision shows death being conquered and abolished. The vision shows all of the acts of the flesh being judged—this is the prerequisite to life in the spirit. Viewed in this way, the lake of fire is part of the great victory of Christ over evil for which every faithful heart has yearned. Nations and generations of individuals will indeed be placed under the torment and burden of subjection to righteous rule. But, in this state of subjugation, the torment in the experience of each individual will be what is needed to burn out the structure of the lie, that the realization of the truth might be fully founded and built up and become a bulwark for faith.

THE NEW HEAVEN AND NEW EARTH

The repetition of the words *heaven* and *earth*, and the labeling of each one as *new* and *former* in the first verse of chapter 21, creates a momentary pause in the vision that is demanded by the awe-inspiring events that take place. The former heaven and earth pass away in fire (2 Pet. 3:7, 10-13). This is a great eonian transition. Everything will be different from what it was before. Politics will be replaced with the knowledge of God. All strife and conflict, every cause of grief, all that is false, will be eliminated. In Genesis man was driven from the garden of God, but in the new heaven and on the new earth, God will dwell with mankind.

The Sea Is No More

The sea stands alone in contrast here (Rev. 21:1). The *new heaven* and *new earth* are accented by parallel contrast with *former heaven* and *former earth*. What is the import of the absence of the sea? This may be a contrast with earth's conditions during previous eons when sin, death and ruin were part of the norm. The earth was overflowed with water in the opening of Genesis and also during Noah's flood. These conditions were the results of judgment upon sin. God set bounds to hold back the sea's proud waves of destruction (Job 38:8-11) providing a habitable place for humanity. From this viewpoint the absence of the sea suggests the idea that no longer is there a chance of passing under an overwhelming judgment, and that death and ruin will have no place on the new earth. This agrees with the decree from the great white throne (vv. 3-5).

In some instances the *sea* (*thalassa*) and the *submerged chaos*, or, *abyss* (*abussos*) seem to be interchangeable terms. The wild beast ascends out of the sea (Rev. 13:1), and also is said to ascend out of the abyss (Rev. 11:7; 17:8). The abyss is where the demon—locusts are locked (Rev. 9:1-3). Some think this is the same as Tartarus (2 Pet. 2:4). While the abyss may appear to be a prison for spiritual beings, at other times it seems to refer to the oceans or to subterranean waters (Gen. 1:2; 7:11; 8:2; Ex. 15:5; Ps. 104:6; etc.). Yet in other instances it occurs as a symbolic term for death, as in Romans 10:7, "...Who will be descending into the submerged chaos [*abussos*]?—that is, to be leading Christ up from among the dead." The Hebrew thought behind these expressions may have been that the measure of descent is the measure of separation from God, thereby expressing the degree of alienation from Him. The expression "lower parts of the earth" (Eph. 4:9; Ezek. 3:14, 16, 18; 32:18, 24; Ps. 88:4-7; cf. also Jonah 2:2-7), though requiring no thought of water, is a similar expression, which may also suggest death. The seas simply form in the lowest parts of the earth because of gravity. The point here is that the sea is linked to the ideas of death, condemnation and separation from God. The sea will be no more, because those conditions suggested by it will be no more.

The sea may also be seen as a feature of this earth that is subject to the power of the air. The winds of the atmosphere can move upon the water and whip it up into treacherous billowing waves. Examples of this may be found in Mark 4:37, Luke 8:23, Jonah 1:4 and also in Daniel 7:2, which is part of Daniel's vision where the beasts came up out of the sea. Wind and spirit are the same word in the biblical languages.

Thus the wind may be viewed as a spiritual force moving waters, and waters are sometimes typical of the nations of the earth. Examples where raging nations are spoken of as billows of the sea are not uncommon (Jer. 51:42; Ps. 65:7; 89:9, 10; Ezek. 26:3-5; etc.). The thousand years end with the Adversary inciting the nations into a billowing wave of rebellion to overflow the citadel of the saints (Rev. 20:7-9). From the perspective of these thoughts, the absence of the sea in Revelation 21:1 suggests that this volatile feature of humanity has been stilled. And it could also mean that through the judgment upon spiritual beings, they will no longer affect humanity in such a way. Those of humanity who are perfected are no longer lower than the messengers. Indeed, the body of Christ will be judging messengers (1 Cor. 6:3). And in becoming sons of God, humanity will be equal with the messengers (Lk. 20:36). Humanity will not always be subject to the influence of the spiritual realm. During the final eon with a new heaven and a new earth the creation will "be freed from the slavery of corruption into the glorious freedom of the children of God" (Rom. 8:21). All of the things mentioned in Revelation 21:1-4 are those things for which "the entire creation is groaning and travailing" (Rom. 8:22). It is a great liberation that is coming.

The Edict from the Throne

"And I hear a loud voice out of the throne saying, 'Lo! the tabernacle of God is with mankind, and He will be tabernacling with them, and they will be His peoples, and God Himself will be with them. And He will be brushing away every tear from their eyes. And death will be no more, nor mourning, nor clamor, nor misery; they will be no more, for the former things passed away.'

"And He Who is sitting on the throne said, 'Lo! New am I making all!'" (Rev. 21:3-5).

The tabernacling of God is the first feature of this edict. He is not said to be tabernacling with the saints, or Israel, or the bride, or the Church, or the body of Christ, or even the overcomers. Through most of this book the faithful ones receive the notice, due to the theme of the book. But here the prospect is looking forward to what will be accomplished in that final eon. Now "the tabernacle of God is with mankind, and He will be tabernacling with them, and they will be His peoples, and God Himself will be with them." There will be no more chance of being driven from God's presence, as Adam and Eve were from Eden. The expression of God being *with* humanity is repeated three times, emphasizing the final goal that will be reached, and that God *Himself* ensures its accomplishment.

Next is the mention of tears, death, mourning, clamor, misery, and all such former things. These things are *former* because they came to humanity under the headship of Adam. When this vision is fulfilled, all, humanity and the spiritual realm as well, will be under the Headship of Christ. The prophetic curse of Genesis 3 introduced all these *former* things to humanity. Christ delivers humanity from them. He Who is the Firstborn of all creation is also the Firstborn from among the dead. He is the Beginning of the new creation as well, and He is the Promise that all will be made new.

The Holy City, New Jerusalem

"And I perceived the holy city, new Jerusalem, descending out of heaven from God, made ready as a bride adorned for her husband" (Rev. 21:2). The nation which had been a harlot, and divorced from God in the Hebrew prophecies is now renewed and experiencing the joy of a bride. Hannah's song is fulfilled in its relation to the nation of Israel. Rachel's *son of sorrow*, born at Bethlehem, has become *son of the right hand* (Gen. 35:16-19). In the days of David the citadel of Zion was captured, and the city of Jerusalem built up. Here in John's vision the citadel of the saints was surrounded, but the protection of God was manifested (Rev. 20:7-10) and now new Jerusalem is established in unprecedented glory.

Is the new Jerusalem a glorious city built of gold and precious stones? Many say it is. Is the new Jerusalem a people, the bride? Is the new Jerusalem both a glorified people and the structure of a city in which the structure matches the glorified characteristics of the people? We believe the third question merits the answer, yes. Pre-eminently in view are the people, the saints. Still, Jerusalem is the choice figure to express all the things associated with these people. *Jerusalem* means *the occupation* or *possession of peace*. The city will never live up to that name until it comes on the new earth. Yet Jerusalem stands as a figure for many generations of Jews—many lives of faith. It ties them all together. The saints will function from the holy, royal city, new Jerusalem. The city will be the location or focal point of their action. The description of the city is one with the description of its people. The people are "a kingdom and a priesthood for our God, and they shall be reigning on the earth" (Rev. 5:10; 1:6).

Reigning, or, *rule* presupposes alienation or insubjection in the social realm. Priesthood presupposes alienation from and insubjection to God. The new Jerusalem is the reborn Israel, functioning as mediators between God and humanity. The Jewish nation will fulfill the promise to Abraham in a way additional to the sacrifice of Christ—administrating His headship. Through the mediation of Abraham's seed, all families of the earth will be blessed (Gen. 12:3).

Perfection is not reached with the coming of the new heaven and new earth. Perfection will be reached through the completion of the reign of Christ. Christ must reign *until* all enemies are placed under His feet (1 Cor. 15:25). When Christ becomes the head of all, delegated authority will all be nullified, having become obsolete (1 Cor. 15:24). The bride, the new Jerusalem of John's vision, is exercising delegated authority by reigning and performing the ministry of priests. Thus, as long as the saints are administrating the affairs of the kingdom, the second death still holds many. Death is the last enemy, and it will be abolished (1 Cor. 15:26), but that abolition will not be complete until the last one held in the second death has been made immortal. The second death continues to exist on the new earth, and the second death is the reason for the ministry of the kingdom of priests. When the second death ceases to exist, there will no longer be a need for rule or for priests.

The Wall

God chose Israel "to belong to Him as a special people above all the peoples who are on the surface of the ground" (Deut. 14:2). Because God chose them to be a special people to Him, Israel was given restrictions—the law and covenants—that made them separate from the world in many ways. Israel's separation from the world is still emphasized in the 21st chapter of Revelation, but it has taken on a whole new character. In the description of the new Jerusalem, its wall is mentioned six times (Rev. 21:12, 14, 15, 17, 18, 19). Walls separate. When Paul spoke of the unity of the new humanity, he said that the dividing wall was razed (Eph. 2:14). But John's vision does not reach far enough into the future to show the ultimate outcome of all that Paul revealed. It is, however, the next closest step, because of the nature of this wall.

This wall is different because it has open access in every direction, and that access is never closed (Rev. 21:12-14, 25). This wall is different because its twelve foundations are not the fathers of the nation that lives there, but the twelve foundations are the apostles of the One Who is the greatest Revelation of God that humanity has ever been given (Rev. 21:14).

This wall is different because it is transparent, made of crystalline jasper (Rev. 21:11, 18). Jasper is essentially quartz. It is found in many colors—red, green, brown, black. Organic materials within the quartz give it these colors. As long as these colors remain in the jasper, it is opaque. The light cannot pass through it. But the jasper of the walls of the bride have had all the colorings of the previous life purified and removed. The strength and purpose and motives of this mighty wall are all clear as crystal. Quartz crystal is glorified jasper. The new Jerusalem is glorified people.

Do Those in the Lake of Fire Have Access to the Water of Life?

Who is allowed to drink from the river of water of life and partake of the log, or tree of life? Do only those who were believers or were awarded life at the great white throne judgment partake of this water? Are those in the second death allowed to drink of these blessings? It is very easy to misunderstand these final chapters, because John's viewpoint changes repeatedly. He changes freely from narrating the vision to describing things about the vision.

"To him who is thirsting I shall be giving of the spring of the water of life gratuitously. He who is conquering shall be enjoying this allotment, and I shall be a God to him and he shall be a son to Me. Yet the timid, and unbelievers, and the abominable, and murderers, and paramours, and enchanters, and idolaters, and all the false—their part is in the lake burning with fire and sulphur, which is the second death" (Rev. 21:6-8)

Upon the first reading of these verses, one receives the impression that the water of life is only for those of faith. But closer examination shows access to be much broader. In verse 6 the perspective changes from viewing John's vision to speaking of the vision's blessings from the prospect of the day in which John was living. In verses 9-21 he returns to viewing the vision of the new Jerusalem. Notice then, in verses 6 and 7, a twofold description of those who will definitely enjoy these blessings: (1) they were thirsting, and, (2) they would be conquering. This does not describe what their condition will be when the new Jerusalem arrives. It describes their condition and actions of faith in the days when they lived by faith and were told of these blessings in John's prophecy. Notice also that their thirst was slacked from a spring of the water of life, not a river. The faithful ones thirsted in the days of their lives when they heard the prophecy of John's vision, and they conquered in the days when they were persecuted. When the new Jerusalem comes they will not thirst, and they will not need to conquer, because the battle will already be won. Their access is free and unrestricted.

Similarly those who are "timid, and unbelievers, and the abominable…" fit these descriptions in the times prior to the great white throne judgment. On the new earth, those who are described here have been resurrected from the dead to stand before the great white throne. God has judged them and pronounced their sentence. They are certainly not yet perfected, but they have been through experiences too traumatic to think that their behavior will remain unaltered. At this point it may seem that the blessings are only for believers, but the situation is unfolded more as John supplies details on life after the description of the new Jerusalem.

"And a temple I did not perceive in it, for the Lord God almighty is its temple, and the Lambkin. And the city has no need of the sun nor of the moon, that they should be appearing in it, for the glory of God illuminates it, and its lamp is the Lambkin.

"And the nations shall be walking by means of its light, and the kings of the earth are carrying their glory into it. And its portals should under no circumstances be locked by day; for there shall be no night there. And they shall be carrying the glory and the honor of the nations into it, and under no circumstances may anything contaminating, or one who is making an abomination and a lie be entering into it, except those written in the Lambkin's scroll of life" (Rev. 21:22-27).

Here it is affirmed that only those written in the Lambkin's scroll of life may enter into the city, but there is also more information given regarding those outside the city. Who are the nations outside the city? These will be of a considerable variety. These nations would include those that were subject to Israel during the millennium, those who had been judged favorably at the great white throne, and those in the second death. Paul said in 1 Corinthians 15 that those who were Christ's would be vivified at His presence. This indicates that all those with access to the city have been changed and are immortal. The great white throne judges individuals, but the context here speaks of nations, so there will probably be a wide degree of difference in the condition of those individuals of the nations who are outside.

"The nations shall be walking by means of its light." That is, the nations shall be walking in accordance with the light of God's glory as it was manifested through the Lambkin.

Clearly this means that they will walk in an orderly way, pleasing to God. They do not yet have access within the city, but their behavior is vastly improved and under control.

"And he shows me a river of water of life, resplendent as crystal, issuing out of the throne of God and the Lambkin. In the center of its square, and on either side of the river, is the log of life, producing twelve fruits, rendering its fruit in accord with each month. And the leaves of the log are for the cure of the nations. (compare Ps.46)

"And there shall be no more any doom, and the throne of God and of the Lambkin shall be in it. And His slaves shall be offering divine service to Him. And they shall be seeing His face, and His name shall be on their foreheads. And night shall be no more, and they have no need of lamplight and sunlight, for the Lord God shall be illuminating them. And they shall be reigning for the eons of the eons" (Rev. 22:1-5).

In verse 1, the water of life now is manifested as a river, issuing from the throne of God and the Lambkin. It is no longer a spring, as it was when revealed to those who believed on the old earth, and who conquered then through the blood of the Lambkin. Since the river issues from the throne, rule is in view. And the rule is the river. And the rule flows out to the world. The river is for the world, not those inside. God's slaves are serving Him (v. 3). His slaves are kings and priests (1 Pet. 2:9; Rev. 1:6; 5:10; 20:4, 6; 22:5), reigning with Christ. The bride, new Jerusalem, is the people who are reigning. The water of life is their allotment (21:7). As their allotment, it is their tenancy—they work it. It is not something they possess only for their own satisfaction. The river of life is what they do as they reign and minister as priests. The Spirit of God is within them, they had thirsted before, and now, out of their hearts flow rivers of living water (Jn.7:37). They are the dwelling of God, and God's life flows out through them to those in need. They are seated with Christ in His throne. The throne of God is within them and rule flows out of them. They are kings because they rule over those who are not yet fully subject to God. They are priests because they function in a mediatory capacity to complete reconciliation to God. This is their allotment.

The square of the city was mentioned a few verses before: "the square of the city is gold, clear as translucent glass" (Rev. 21:21). The square of the city is the place of commerce and social interaction—the marketplace of the city. It is not the idea of superfluous wealth, so often attributed to the highly celebrated "streets of gold," but it is the thought of true motives, divine motives, in the hearts of all the citizens. In social interaction there are no hidden agendas—no ulterior motives—no deceptive practices. There is the simplicity and honesty of children, combined with the love and concern of mature adults. This is one reason why entrance to the city is still limited—not yet have all been brought to that unity with God. Access to the city does not represent membership in the most prestigious of clubs with inestimable wealth. Access to the city represents the highest plane of intimacy and openness with God. There is no temple there, because the Lord God Almighty is there and is the temple, and the Lambkin with Him (Rev. 21:22). Those who minister the rule and life of God to others are the ones with access to the city. They are taking out to the world of humanity what they enjoy within.

The things inside the city are needed by those outside the city. The leaves are for the cure or healing of the nations. The divine service that God's slaves offer to Him is to serve, like the Lambkin did. As kings and priests to the world they administer the blessings of the city to those outside.

"The throne of God and the Lambkin shall be in it" (v. 3). This marks a change. John perceived a great white throne (Rev. 20:11). It was ***a*** throne, not ***the*** throne. But, in the five following occurrences of the word throne (20:12; 21:3, 5; 22:1, 3), it is ***the*** throne, showing that it refers back to the great white throne. Christ said, "The one who is conquering, to him will I be granting to be seated with Me on My throne as I, also, conquer, and am seated with My Father on His throne" (Rev. 3:21). Humanity was judged at the great white throne, apart from the city of new Jerusalem. But subsequently the throne takes its place in the city. This defines the city, the bride, as the seat of God's authority and rule and the seat of most sacred holiness.

This is described as a final stage of the fulfillment of God's covenant with Abraham. The seat of authority is not owned by God and the Lambkin only, but is shared with all those who make up the bride. All families of the earth will be blessed through the rule and ministry of God's chosen ones. Notice the things said about God's slaves: they "shall be offering divine service to Him, they shall be seeing His face, His name shall be in their foreheads, the Lord God shall be illuminating them, they shall be reigning for the eons of the eons."

"And they shall be reigning for the eons of the eons" (Rev. 22:5). With this statement, it can be seen that John's perspective changes again. He does not only speak of the condition of things on the new earth. He includes also the millennial eon previous to that time—"the eons of the eons." This is followed by a statement of the truth of the things prophesied in these visions, and then he says, "Happy is he who is keeping the sayings of the prophecy of this scroll." The time element has reverted to John's day, and is no longer in the future eons. This brings us again to a context that is often confused because of the time frame we may try to place it in. "Happy are those who are rinsing their robes, that it will be their license to the log of life, and they may be entering the portals into the city. Outside are curs, and enchanters, and paramours, and murderers, and idolaters, and everyone fabricating and fondling falsehood" (Rev. 22:14, 15). In Exodus 19:10, when the people were preparing to enter into covenant with God, they first had to rinse their robes. The rinsing of robes takes place in John's day, or the current day in which one hears of Christ and believes. Those who are labeled curs, enchanters, idolaters, murderers, etc., are guilty of those things in life previous to the great white throne. This passage is not saying that those sins are being committed on the new earth outside of the city. The nations at that time will walk according to the light of the city.

THE HEADSHIP OF CHRIST

The Administration of the Complement of the Eras

"...in accord with His delight...to have an administration of the complement of the eras, to head up all in the Christ—both that in the heavens and that on the earth..." (Eph. 1:9-10)

It is God's delight to make those whom He has called in grace part of an administration. This administration will function during the complement of the eras. That is, it will function during the final eras which complete or fill up the remaining time periods in the eons. These eras will cover the times of the great white throne judgment, the coming of the new heavens and earth, and whatever eras remain until the consummation, when all are made immortal through Christ. Reborn Israel will be the element of this administration on the earth, and the body of Christ, whose "realm is inherent in the heavens" (Phil. 3:20), will be the element of this administration located there.

The eons of the eons are the final two eons revealed in the scriptures. As these eons progress through their various eras, the glory poured out at the feet of Christ and wafting up to the Father will continually increase. A hiker, traveling through the forest to a great waterfall, becomes aware, almost subconsciously, of a low and distant sound. As he draws closer to the fall, the sound of breaking water becomes louder and louder. Finally, standing at the bottom of the fall, the crescendo has swelled to a deafening roar that vibrates the very air the hiker breathes. Like the sound of a great waterfall, the glory to Christ and God will continually increase through the course of the final eons, until every being is singing in full-hearted praise, and the entire creation resonates with joy and exhilaration.

The scriptures are clear that this is an apt appraisal of the final outcome. For this to be true, the number of humanity becoming reconciled to God must be increasing throughout the eon of the eons. But if the second death were literal death, no such progression in glory would be possible. If all who did not receive eonian life at the great white throne were dead, no one would be reconciled to God during the final eon! If all who were not judged for life at the great white throne were literally dead, the kingdom of priests would be on holiday for the eon of the eons. There would be none but those like the queen of the south and the repentant Ninevites to be ruled and receive ministry.

If the second death is figurative, then all those judged at the great white throne will live under subjection, but in circumstances that lead to the glorious liberty of the children of God (Rom. 8:19-22). As their judgment is fulfilled, in each day and each experience, they will be coming to a greater realization of the truth, and their honor and praise of God will continually grow, till it reaches completion in their vivification. A figurative understanding of the second death accords well with the concept of the glory of God and Christ continually increasing through the course of the final eras. And a figurative understanding of the second death accords well with the teachings that all will be subjected to Christ and come under His Headship.

Paul and John on Eschatology

Paul sheds more light on the final eon and its outcome than any other writer in the Greek scriptures (see 1 Cor. 15:20-28; Eph. 1-3 etc.). Yet, in some ways, his revelations are more difficult to grasp (not that John's are easy). Paul speaks with words deep and powerful and complex, challenging the mind. John speaks in figures and images that carry the heart aloft, but sometimes leave the understanding behind. We need them both. We need both the inspiration and the depth of understanding. We need both the exhilaration that is felt when standing on the pinnacle of the structure, and we also need the master-builder's foundation.

John: Rule in the Final Eon

Not only will Israel be the head of the nations, but Israelites will probably be designated as heads of the foreign nations, and will administrate over the personnel responsible for the rule in each nation. The nations will be carrying their glory and honor into the new Jerusalem (Rev. 21:26), but it is only those who are written in the Lamb's scroll of life that will be entering into the city. Even the closing verses of John's vision emphasize Israel's enjoyment of the blessings to the neglect of the blessing that will flow through Israel's ministry. This accords with the theme of the book—*be faithful through trial, because victory is coming*. This does not mean that the blessings are limited to Israel and the faithful. They will be the dispensers. But their current trials and the theme of the book call for the blessings of the chosen ones to be emphasized.

There are four outstanding figures in the closing verses of Revelation that speak volumes about rule on the new earth during the final eon. They are the Lambkin, the light, the river and the log of life. Notice that all four of these refer to rule.

The Lambkin and Rule

The Concordant Version uses the term *lambkin* for *arnion*. *Amnos* is the usual word for *lamb* (as in Jn. 1:29; Acts 8:32; etc.). *Arnion* is the diminutive form, emphasizing the idea of smallness, or, in this case of the lamb, it carries the idea of harmlessness to a further degree. *Arnion* occurs only once in the Bible besides in the book of Revelation (Jn. 21:15). In Revelation it occurs twenty-nine times, twenty-eight of which refer to the Lord.

Lambkin is a good translation to carry the emphasis of the original language into English, but, in the context of the book, it sometimes takes on the character of an oxymoron. It is the Lion of the tribe of Judah that conquers to open the scroll and loose its seven seals, but He is seen as the Lambkin when He opens it (Rev. 5:5-9). The indignation, or wrath of the Lambkin is mentioned in 6:16. Those worshiping the wild beast and its image will be tormented in the sight of the Lambkin (Rev. 14:9-10). The Lambkin will battle with and conquer the nations that make up the beast (Rev. 17:13-14). Clearly the Lambkin does things that are not usually associated with the character of a lamb. But there is also the emphasis upon the blood and sacrifice of the Lambkin (Rev.

5:12; 12:11), by virtue of which there exists *the Lambkin's scroll of life* (Rev. 13:8; 21:27).

The seeming contradiction disappears in Revelation 12:11 where those who overcome are said to conquer by the blood of the Lambkin and through the word of their testimony. It is clearly the power of God, operating through the sacrifice of Christ, that wins the victory. The figure of the Lambkin is a constant reminder that the source of power and strength is not in Christ Himself but in the Father.

In the days of Samuel Israel repented and was seeking to return to God. Samuel offered "one milk-fed lambkin" (1 Sam. 7:9 CV), as a whole burnt offering. While he was making the sacrifice, the Philistines were advancing to battle Israel, and God caused thundering over the Philistines that was so loud it shook their confidence, and they fled before the Israelites. The Israelites recaptured their cities and enjoyed a long respite from Philistine oppression. This is an example of the power of God manifested through weakness which is dedicated to Him.

The rule of the final eon issues from "the throne of God and the Lambkin" (Rev. 22:1, 3). This is the rule of God in which the sacrifice of His Son is pre-eminent. Every aspect of rule is relative to the sacrifice of Christ. The rule of the final eon is based upon the greatest revelation of the love of God. There can be no fear with regard to this rule or its outcome.

The Light and Rule

"And the city has no need of the sun nor of the moon, that they should be appearing in it, for the glory of God illuminates it, and its lamp is the Lambkin.

"And the nations shall be walking by means of its light, and the kings of the earth are carrying their glory into it. And its portals should under no circumstances by locked by day; for there shall be no night there" (Rev. 21:23-25).

What is the light mentioned in these verses? Light is used extensively in the Bible as a figure for other things—knowledge, truth, wisdom, godliness. Here we are told that the nations "shall be walking by means of its light"—by means of the light of the holy city, new Jerusalem. It is the light of the bride—the people.

The light here is rule. It controls how the nations behave—how they walk. The nations will walk according to the truth. The rule that is extant at that time will ensure that they do. The office of the people of new Jerusalem is also in the function of priests. Therefore the knowledge of God is inherently part of this light.

Guidance comes to mind as an apt description of this rule. Light enables one to see, and thereby guides one's course. And certainly this light goes beyond guidance too. The nations are said to carry their glory into this city. This means that they are bringing the things to it that manifest the giving of honor to God. Honoring God can only truly be done where there is a realization of truth. So the rule of this light is such that it imparts the knowledge of the truth to those who are ruled by it.

The River and Rule

"And he shows me a river of water of life, resplendent as crystal, issuing out of the throne of God and the Lambkin. In the center of its square, and on either side of the river, is the log of life..." (Rev. 22:1, 2).

The river issues from the throne of God and the Lambkin. Since the source of the river is the throne, the river is a description of the rule during the final eon. The river is "water of life." The rule of the final eon is a rule that brings life to all under its authority. Those who are under the authority of this rule are all those from the great white throne judgment. Some of those received life, and are enjoying the blessings of such a glorious rule. Many from that judgment will go to the lake of fire, the second death. They will be learning subjection to Christ under a government which will refresh them from the trial of their subjugation, and which will slack the thirst caused by the second death with life—resplendent, clear as crystal, water of life. The rule that issues from the throne of God and the Lambkin is so described with such terms of beauty and refreshment and renewal that it is certainly a rule which would cause one to say, "It is a good thing, to be alive!" Such a statement would come from the lips of those who came from the grave, after experiencing every manner of *life* that could have been described as anything but life. On both sides of the river is the log or tree of life. We are intended to see the river and trees as parts of a single picture—aspects of one rule.

The Log of Life and Rule

"In the center of its square, and on either side of the river, is the log of life, producing twelve fruits, rendering its fruit in accord with each month. And the leaves of the log are for the cure of the nations" (Rev. 22:2).

The word which the Concordant Version renders *log* here is *xulon*, which means *wood. Xulon* is used to designate such things as the cross on which Christ was crucified, wood as a building material (1 Cor. 3:12), the *stocks* in which Paul's feet were fastened in prison (Acts 16:24), staffs or clubs (Matt. 26:47), and other wooden articles. *Dendron* is the biblical word for *tree*. It is used frequently in referring to living trees.

The beautiful figure employed here is that of resurrection life. The wood was dead, but is alive again and is a source of continual sustenance. The previous life was cut off, and now is replaced by one of superior vitality. "Then a Twig will come forth from the set slip of Jesse, and a Scion, it shall be fruitful from his roots" (Isa. 11:1). The house of David was long cut off. The nation of Israel was figuratively dead and scattered among the nations, but the kingdom is resurrected under Christ, the Lamb.

Where is such a tree that can produce twelve fruits? Where is such a tree that produces fruit every month? Where is a tree that also produces leaves that have healing power? All of this must refer to the resurrection life of Christ, provided for all on the dead wood of the cross of Golgotha—the dead wood of crucified flesh.

Aaron was designated as chief priest, and the tribe of Levi affirmed as the priestly tribe by God's miracle performed on Aaron's staff of wood. The staff of each of the heads of the twelve tribes was taken, and their name was written on it. Aaron represented Levi. Moses placed all the staffs in the tabernacle before God. The next day all the staffs were the same as before, except for Aaron's. It had buds and blossoms and almond fruit (Num. 17). The resurrection confirms the Headship of Christ. But He is not just the Head of a tribe or nation, He is the Head of the race, replacing Adam in that position (1 Cor. 15:20-24; Rom. 5:12-21; Eph. 1:9-10, 22-23; 1 Cor. 11:3; etc.). As Head of all, He is the source of life for all.

The log of life is stamped with the number twelve, the number of rule, in two ways. It produces twelve fruits, and it produces them in twelve months. Months are a lunar designation. The moon, the lesser light, was for the rule of darkness, or night (Gen. 1:5, 16). So the thought of rule is associated with the log of life. Emphasized here especially is the thought of the rule of those who have not yet fully come into the light. Those who are still in some shade of darkness need the healing of the leaves and the sustaining fruit of life. Yet this is a temporary need. This too is insinuated where we are told there is no night there. The lesser light for those in darkness is giving way to the greater light. This speaks especially of those of the second death who are not yet fully subject to Christ. They do not yet realize Him as their Head.

The log of life is in the center of the square of the new Jerusalem, as well as on either side of the river. This location identifies it with the central purpose of the city and of the rule that issues from the city. That purpose is to give life. So, while these blessings are specifically promised to those faithful ones undergoing persecution, there can be no doubt that those persecuted ones will take on the character and mission of their Head, Who is described as the Lambkin, the life-giving sacrifice. The simple presence of those needing the cure provided by the leaves is another confirmation that those of the second death are not literally dead. And the thought of healing shows that all the needs of every individual will be met. Subjection to God and alienation from Him are the only aspects of the ministry of His servants.

Universal Subjection to Christ's Headship

"Wherefore, also, God highly exalts Him, and graces Him with the name that is above every name, that in the name of Jesus every knee should be bowing, celestial and terrestrial and subterranean, and every tongue should be acclaiming that Jesus Christ is Lord, for the glory of God the Father" (Phil. 2:9-11).

How does this grand climax of the eons come about? Is this passage speaking of a final time when the last ones of humanity and the spiritual beings come to a realization of the truth and offer their heartfelt devotion and allegiance to Christ? Yes, that will happen, and that time will surely come and fulfill this scripture. But may it also be looking beyond that to a first ever assembly of all rational beings bowing in unison before the Lord Jesus, and acclaiming His Lordship over them? That also may occur. What a cause for celebration!

It seems almost paradoxical that Christ should rule until all are subjected to Him, yet when He reaches that goal, He will cease ruling, abdicate His throne, and hand back to His Father a completed and unified creation. So when Christ is finally and fully Lord of all, He stops being Lord. And a grand and glorious event, which seems very much like a coronation ceremony, leads into an abdication of the throne.

At the great white throne, we noted that popular view which tends to make it the great white dais, or, judgment seat. Judgment is meted out. But we saw that the great white throne was indeed a throne, because decrees come forth from it and rule flows from it during the final eon. All of the governing and political aspects that would be expected from such a throne will indeed issue forth. But when Christ becomes Lord of all, then the need for rule will cease to exist, and all delegated offices of rule and authority will be abolished. Perhaps *then* the great white throne will become a great white dais. Every rational creature will voice their judgment that the Son of God is worthy to rule all. Then the Son of God will remove all the diadems of authority from His brow and place them at the Father's feet. And the Father will pass His final act of judgment as He announces that the work of His Son is *very good*. And every heart watching will know what is going to happen. Every eye will see the Son and rejoice to see Him honored. But every heart will know that He will not hold on to that glorious honor, because He has already laid it all aside once before.

Conclusion on the Second Death

Death is the cessation of life. The first death is a condition in which there is no consciousness. There is no sensation, no awareness of the passing of time, no awareness of anything in the first death. But the second death is announced in John's vision as a condition in which there is consciousness and torment. And this torment extends for long indefinite periods of time. There must be a significant difference in definition of the first death and the second death.

What is the lake of fire? The lake of fire was part of a scene in a vision of the apostle John. This lake of fire was the place of incarceration and chastisement for grotesque creatures which represented world-dominating political systems in the vision, and for personified figures for death and hades. When Christ returns in glory and power, He will bring all the political systems of this world to their knees. They will be subjected to the rule of the reborn, priestly nation of Israel. There will be a world-wide reign of strict justice and righteousness. The servitude and chastisement to which the nations will be subject during this reign is the literal reality that was figuratively shown as a lake of fire in John's vision. The lake of fire-—the second death is not literal death.

The millennial period of strict rule is a display that humanity cannot live in peace apart from receiving the Spirit of God. Even righteous government is insufficient to cure the ills of the world. Satan will be loosed at the end of the millennium and will immediately bring humanity to war with Christ and the saints. These forces will be summarily vanquished. Then will come the era of the great white throne judgment and the new heaven and earth.

The rule of righteousness will continue on in the new earth, so that those who died previously may receive its benefits and teaching. But the character of the rule will change. Christ, the Sovereign, will not be known as the Lion of the tribe of Judah, but rather as the Lambkin—the reconciling sacrifice. Since the rule over the unbelieving and wicked on the earth during the millennium was seen by John in the vision as a lake of fire, that description is carried over in the vision to rule on the new earth also. All those judged at the great white throne enter the baptism of perfect rule and subjection that brings them to the realization of truth which cleanses their lives. Yet the rule of that final eon changes so dramatically that it must also be described as a river of the water of life. While it has aspects of torment and hardship, still it brings life and satisfaction. Healing is provided for all. Christ's Melchizedekian reign completes both righteousness and peace, until all are made immortal and until there is no longer any need for rule. Finally, all will be given immortality, and death will be abolished. All will realize the truth. Then God will be All in all.

We find then, that the misunderstanding of a prophet's vision misrepresented the awesome cleansing judgments of God as the gruesome results of anger and frustration, as if God could not accomplish His purpose. And we find that the scriptures actually have a great deal to say about the second death. Many of the parables spoken by the Lord refer to that condition, though they do not call it by that name. He came speaking of life and death, and of eonian life and the second death. The second death is a figurative expression that contrasts the existence of those judged at the great white throne with the eonian life of the chosen.

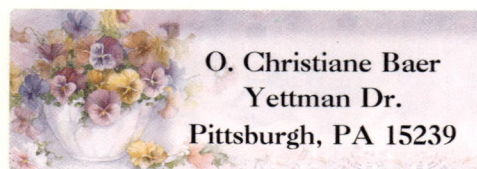

O. Christiane Baer
Yettman Dr.
Pittsburgh, PA 15239

CPSIA information can be obtained at www.ICGtesting.com
Printed in the USA
LVOW10s1121200616

493331LV00001B/47/P

9 781604 773248